NEV

also by Alex Garland

novels

THE BEACH
THE TESSERACT
THE COMA

screenplays

28 DAYS LATER
SUNSHINE

NEVER LET ME GO

Alex Garland

based on the novel by
KAZUO ISHIGURO

ff
faber and faber

First published in 2011
by Faber and Faber Limited
Bloomsbury House
74–77 Great Russell Street
London WC1B 3DA

Typeset by Country Setting, Kingsdown, Kent CT14 8ES
Printed in England by CPI Bookmarque, Croydon, Surrey

A CIP record for this book
is available from the British Library

ISBN 978–0–571–27548–9

2 4 6 8 10 9 7 5 3 1

CONTENTS

INTRODUCTION

Kazuo Ishiguro

Perhaps you've heard that the cafés of North-West London, especially in its leafier districts, are filled with writers in earnest discussion about their work. This of course is largely myth. As any local will testify, it is babies, not writers, who are to be found dominating any place that will serve a cappuccino, passionately exchanging views on their handlers, food, the latest milestone passed. Though fully aware of this, Alex Garland and I, often together with novelist William Sutcliffe, have been trying for many years now to live the myth of those writers' gatherings, battling valiantly against the superior vocal powers of our rival faction. One reward for our efforts, you could say, is the book you are now holding: the film adaptation of *Never Let Me Go* was yet another infant that passed through its early developmental stages in those cafés.

I first met Alex in the spring of 1998 in a tiny café in England's Lane shortly after the publication of his backpacking classic, *The Beach* – a novel I had mightily enjoyed. He was in his twenties then, with traces of an adolescent awkwardness still in his posture, but also the assurance peculiar to the unusually talented. He looked like he hadn't slept for days, and ordered Diet Cokes at such a rate the waiter suspected a prank. His imagination seemed to be on fire with ideas and projects, but when he talked, his delivery was controlled, almost halting. I noticed how carefully he watched and listened; how he would weigh up each thing I said, before coming back with a considered, sometimes mildly confrontational response. He was terrific company.

We got into the habit of meeting for lunch every two or three months. The babies sometimes forced us to retreat to the periphery, into eerie restaurants on the brink of bankruptcy. But we went on swapping views on anything and everything, and I can see now this was where the first part of our collaboration on *Never Let Me Go* really began. I had started to write the novel in early 2001, and would often run ideas past him, without explaining their context or even that they related to my work. Alex's responses were always thought-provoking, sometimes inspiring. And then there was the science-fiction.

We discussed J.G. Ballard, Alan Moore; the films of Ridley Scott, Cronenberg, Kubrick. He made me a list of the essential graphic novels I had to read and explained the strengths and weaknesses of that form. Most memorably, he brought to my house one afternoon a first draft of a sci-fi horror screenplay he'd just finished, one that would become *28 Days Later*, a film that would top the US box office and make him one of the most sought-after writers in the movie industry. It struck me that while my own generation of so-called literary novelists (I am fifteen years older than Alex) regarded science-fiction with instinctive suspicion, many of Alex's looked to it with excitement, as a rich source of enticing conceits and new ways to pose big old questions such as 'What does it mean to be human?' or 'What does it mean to have a soul?' The sci-fi-derived dystopian setting of *Never Let Me Go* owes an awful lot to those rambling lunches.

When, sometime in 2004, Alex read an uncorrected proof of *Never Let Me Go* and said he'd like to turn it into a screenplay, what I felt more than anything was relief. This was partly because, after all our conversations during the writing of the novel, he'd become in my mind the natural choice for screenwriter. But there was another reason why I was convinced Alex would be the perfect adaptor for the screen.

At a dinner some months earlier, I'd been talking to Alex's publishing editor, Walter Donohue, who'd made the point that Alex's work focused obsessively on characters who had been, in some sense, orphaned: who faced the challenge of working out a new societal or familial system in a threateningly altered, near-Hobbesian world. The teenage backpackers of *The Beach*; the survivors in the post-plague Britain of *28 Days Later*; the astronauts of *Sunshine*, cooped up for years in a spaceship cut off from an earth itself in fear of being orphaned by a fading sun. The parentless world of cloned children trying to make sense of their destiny in *Never Let Me Go* was absolutely Alex Garland territory.

For a time the project remained between the two of us on a handshake basis while Alex concentrated on *Sunshine*, his original screenplay for which an elaborate set was being constructed in East

London. Before long, though, he talked to Andrew MacDonald and Allon Reich at DNA Productions, and contracts were drawn up. Meanwhile the novel was published, and a small, wonderful Chinese restaurant opened adjoining Hampstead Post Office. This now became our regular meeting place and our discussions about *NLMG* continued. At one stage Alex mooted the idea of creating the alternative England we needed by shooting somewhere abroad, where the light would be distinctly un-English. (This idea was ditched as impractical, and in any case, proved unnecessary when Mark Romanek's brilliantly personal eye achieved exactly the desired effect with genuine English locations.)

Something else we discussed (if you're unfamiliar with the story, here comes a mild spoiler) concerned the question: why don't the protagonists ever try to run away? The novel had left this question provocatively – for some readers, annoyingly – unaddressed. Should the film version try to supply some answers? Should we have our characters contemplate – even attempt – escape? Should the film create an infrastructure of physical control absent in the novel? Whenever we returned to this topic, I could sense neither of us had any enthusiasm for it. Alex was no more interested than I had been to tell yet another story of slaves and brave rebellions. What fascinated us both was the astonishing extent to which people, throughout history, have not tried to run away; the degree to which they have accepted, sometimes with sad dignity and courage, horrible marriages, demeaning and dangerous jobs, dictatorships, orders to charge towards enemy guns. Most crucially, we agreed the film had to resonate as a metaphor for the basic human condition – the fact that none of us, ultimately, can run away from death, and have only a poignantly short time to grapple with such things as love, friendship and forgiveness.

A question that preoccupied Alex much more was: how do we make it moving? I told him this was now his problem, not mine. But we did discuss a lot *what sort* of moving. Once, on one of my less inspired days, I suggested the sadness conveyed at the close of the film shouldn't be one of intense anguish, but rather a qualified, resigned, almost satisfied sadness such as – yes, I said this – when someone dear to you dies at a grand old age, having lived a full and fulfilled life. Perhaps out of politeness, Alex concurred with this notion for a few weeks. Then one day over lunch he told me it was 'bollocks'. In fact what he said was: 'Look. The day my dad dies, however long he lives, even if he's really, really old, it's going to be a disaster. A complete, fucking disaster.' He was, of course, absolutely right.

When Alex did sit down to his first draft, he completed it with alarming speed – I seem to remember he took less than a week. It was to go through many revisions, but that first draft was, in essence, very close to the script that follows. Give or take certain details, he had nailed it in one.

This screenplay, you will observe, uses perhaps one-sixth of the number of words the novel does – possibly even fewer. This reflects one fundamental of adapting from novel to screen: huge hunks must be omitted. The screenwriter must decide not only what is inessential to the new trajectory required by the film, but have the vision to see where large paragraphs of prose can be turned into the often more economical language of cinema: the looks on actors' faces, gestures, potent juxtapositions of image and music. No surprise, then, that many things in the novel will not be found here. But you will also find instances where the compression and cutting has produced sharper, more poignant scenes.

One example is the scene on the deserted beach in Norfolk, where Kathy, Ruth and Tommy have come to see a ruined boat abandoned on the sand. In the original, they look at the boat and reminisce about their childhoods. Only later, on the drive back, do tensions rise, culminating in Ruth suddenly asking the other two to forgive her for a lifetime of obstructing their love. In Alex's version, it all happens in one go, with far fewer words, as they sit there on the sand. The movement of emotions is swifter and cleaner, making for an intensely affecting scene – better, I think, than in the novel. It reads powerfully enough in the script: in performance, in the hands of wonderfully gifted actors against the haunting, windswept backdrop conjured by the film-makers, it is an extraordinary experience.

This is an introduction to the screenplay, not to the finished film. So this isn't the place to talk about the precipices scaled in the years between that first draft and *NLMG*'s unveiling at the Odeon Leicester Square as the opening film of the 2010 London Film Festival; no space either to analyse director Mark Romanek's sublimely resonant style, or to ask how on earth the brilliant cast achieved those achingly nuanced performances. But I want to add one more thing, and it concerns Alex's 'Screenplay By' credit.

Film-making is a delicate, massively collaborative process, and the roles taken by the key participants on any one movie are often far more complex than may be suspected by an outsider. Some screenwriters do indeed write the script, hand it over to the director and thereafter adopt a position, more or less, of a privileged spectator. (In fact 'privileged spectator' describes pretty accurately my own role on this film.) This was not Alex's approach. I've conveyed already, I hope, his centrality during the project's fragile infancy. He remained its driving force throughout the development phase, during the recruiting of director, cast and crew. Once shooting began, his judgement was held in such esteem by those in every department that his presence on set, from morning till night, became an absolute necessity. He was the first person to whom Mark and the actors turned when they wished to discuss the playing of a scene; his counsel was sought regarding art direction, sound design, costumes. In post-production, his view was key to every cutting-room decision. The screenplay credit, even supplemented as it is here with 'Executive Producer', barely begins to cover his contribution.

FOX SEARCHLIGHT PICTURES

DNA FILMS

and

FILM4

present

NEVER LET ME GO

PRINCIPAL CAST

KATHY	Carey Mulligan
TOMMY	Andrew Garfield
RUTH	Keira Knightley
YOUNG KATHY	Isobel Meikle-Small
YOUNG RUTH	Ella Purnell
YOUNG TOMMY	Charlie Rowe
MISS EMILY	Charlotte Rampling
MISS LUCY	Sally Hawkins
MADAME	Nathalie Richard
CHRISSIE	Andrea Riseborough
RODNEY	Domhnall Gleeson

PRINCIPAL CREW

Directed by	Mark Romanek
Screenplay by	Alex Garland
Based on the novel by	Kazuo Ishiguro
Produced by	Andrew Macdonald
	Allon Reich
Executive Producers	Alex Garland
	Kazuo Ishiguro
	Tessa Ross
Cinematography by	Adam Kimmel ASC
Production Designer	Mark Digby
Editor	Barney Pilling
Co-Producer	Richard Hewitt
Associate Producer	Joanne Smith
Music by	Rachel Portman
Music Supervisors	Randall Poster
	George Drakoulias
Costume Designers	Rachael Fleming
	Steven Noble
Casting by	Kate Dowd

NEVER LET ME GO
was shown as the Opening Film
at the London Film Festival on 13 October 2010

Never Let Me Go

Open on:

Black screen.

KATHY
(*voice-over*)

My name is Kathy.

Cut to:

EXT. FIELD – EARLY EVENING

Long shadows as the sun goes down.

A field, by a road, lined with a fence.

Snagged in the barbed wire are hundreds of plastic bags. Refuse and litter, blown by the wind, until they were caught.

KATHY
(*voice-over*)

I'm twenty-six years old, and I've been a carer now for seven years.

By the road, a car is parked up against the grass verge.

Standing by the car, a young woman with blonde hair, Kathy, looks towards the fields.

KATHY
(*voice-over*)

My donors have always tended to do better than expected. They are hardly ever classified as agitated, even before a fourth donation.

Cut to:

INT. OBSERVATION ROOM

The same woman, Kathy, standing at the window of an observation room.

She is absent-mindedly twisting a metal bracelet on her wrist. It is featureless except for an imprinted seven-digit number.

Through the glass, she is watching Nurses and Surgeons prepping a twenty-six-year-old man for operation.

Tommy.

KATHY
(*voice-over*)
I'm not trying to boast. It means a lot to me, being able to do my work well.

INT. OPERATING CHAMBER

Tommy is in the process of being sedated.

He also wears a metal bracelet.

Beside him, an Anaesthetist is inserting a drip into his arm.

KATHY
(*voice-over*)
Especially keeping the donors calm.

INT. OBSERVATION ROOM

Tommy turns his head to look at Kathy.

Their locked gaze is held for a beat.

Then Kathy nods. Very slightly. As if to say: it's okay.

Tommy continues looking a moment longer.

Then the Anaesthetist's drug takes hold. In a few seconds, his eyes have gone heavy, then closed.

KATHY
(*voice-over*)
Anyway, I'm not making any great claims for myself.

Back to:

EXT. FIELD – EARLY EVENING

The plastic bags in the barbed wire snap and rustle in the wind.

KATHY
(*voice-over*)
I understand how other carers can be resentful. They say: she's from Hailsham. No wonder she has a great record. She can pick and choose her own kind.

As we close in on Kathy, leaning against the car, her hair caught and whipped in the same wind . . .

. . . fade in the sound of children playing.

KATHY
(*voice-over*)
And it's true. Hailsham was special. We were lucky. Tommy, Ruth, me. All of us.

Cut to:

EXT. HAILSHAM – DAY

Hailsham School: a large Victorian house, set in flat, empty countryside.

The sky above is bright blue and cloudless. The sun is bright. It is an idyll of early summer.

The extensive grounds of the school are surrounded by high hedgerows. Nothing seems to connect it with the rest of the world except a single grey ribbon of road.

Title:

NEVER LET ME GO

The title is not seen, but is spoken by Tommy.

After a few seconds, a title does appear on the screen:

PART I: HAILSHAM

EXT. HAILSHAM GROUNDS – DAY

In sunlight, two girls, aged twelve, lie on their bellies on a patch in front of the main house.

Both wear the metal bracelets – as do all students at Hailsham, and all other facilities like it.

The grass is strewn with daisies.

One girl has blonde hair. This is Kathy.

The other is dark. This is Ruth.

Kathy is interlocking the stems of the small flowers, frowning in concentration, making a daisy chain.

RUTH

I think one day I'd like . . .

She pauses. Thinking a moment.

RUTH

Four horses. (*Beat.*) No, five. Thunder, Bramble, Daffodil and . . .

She trails off.

RUTH

I don't know all their names. But I'd like five horses. (*Beat.*) The best would be Thunder. He'd be dangerous to ride, so you can't ride him. You can ride Bramble. (*Beat.*) As long as you don't use your crop on him.

KATHY

I wouldn't anyway. I would have thought that's mean.

Kathy makes the last link.

She lifts the daisy chain delicately.

RUTH

Pretty.

KATHY

You have it.

Kathy places it over Ruth's blonde hair . . .

. . . where it looks like it belongs.

RUTH

Look . . .

Kathy follows Ruth's gaze.

By the entrance to the main house, two women have appeared. One is older, in her mid-sixties. This is Miss Emily, the head Guardian of Hailsham.

The other is younger, in her late twenties.

RUTH

Who's that with Miss Emily? Do you think it's the new guardian they were telling us about?

KATHY

Miss Lucy. I think it must be.

RUTH

We haven't had a new guardian for ages.

A moment, as the two girls watch the two women, squinting against the bright sunlight.

RUTH

I wonder if she'll fit in.

Cut to:

EXT. HAILSHAM – DAY

A group of boys in their PE kits run through an outdoor covered walkway, watched by a CCTV camera . . .

EXT. PLAYING FIELDS – DAY

. . . then on to the playing fields, watched by . . .

EXT. ORNATE GATE – CONTINUOUS

. . . a group of girls, watching from the shade of a large ornate gate near the main building.

The girls are joined by Kathy and Ruth.

LAURA

Ruth. Kath. Look – they're going to set off Tommy.

AMANDA

Light blue touch paper and stand well back!

On the playing field, we see the boy they are referring to.

Tommy.

RUTH

He really doesn't suspect a thing.

The girls all laugh – except Kathy.

Kathy watches Tommy with slight concern.

KATHY

He's got his shirt on . . . His favourite polo shirt.

From their vantage point, the girls can now see the boys have started lining up. Two captains have stepped forward and are about to start picking teams.

One of the two captains is Arthur, a sporty boy who feels as alpha male as Tommy feels delta.

The captains start choosing team members. Tommy stands – almost a comical figure, puffing out his chest in order to make himself stand out.

The other boys are noticeably less keen. Chatting, or checking the tightness of their bootlaces.

Even from a distance, we can sense Tommy's shift from bright eagerness to puzzled concern, as four boys are chosen before him . . .

Then five . . . six . . .

RUTH

It's coming. Hold on . . . any moment now . . .

. . . until eventually Tommy is left standing alone.

Realising he hasn't been picked. And isn't going to be picked.

The boys all start sniggering.

RUTH

Seven seconds. Six, five, four, three . . .

And suddenly – before Ruth's countdown can complete – Tommy explodes.

Head is thrown back. Bright red. Shaking. Screaming.

The boys are now laughing openly –

– then start to run away, on to the football pitch.

Leaving Tommy alone, directing his rage at the clear blue sky, arms and legs oddly rigid.

EXT. ORNATE GATE – CONTINUOUS

The girls watch, a mixture of transfixed and absently amused by this strange sight.

RUTH

I suppose it is a bit cruel, the way they work him up like that. But it's his own fault. If he learned to keep his cool, they'd leave him alone.

Ruth looks to Kathy, as if for approval –

– but doesn't get it.

Kathy has stood up, and is walking away from the gate towards Tommy.

EXT. PLAYING FIELDS – CONTINUOUS

Kathy approaches Tommy, who is panting from the exertion of his tantrum, still gazing up at the sky.

Kathy puts a hand on Tommy's arm –

– and Tommy recoils violently, throwing his arm up, knocking her hand aside and striking the side of her face.

The strike is an accident – a reaction of surprise and confusion more than anger – but Tommy seems even more shocked than Kathy by what he has done.

A beat.

KATHY

Isn't that your favourite shirt?

Tommy says nothing.

KATHY

I just wanted to say, you shouldn't play football in that shirt. You'll only cover it in mud.

TOMMY

(*mumbling, a little stunned*)

So what? It's nothing to do with you anyway.

Tommy starts to walk away. Kathy watches him go.

EXT. ORNATE GATE – CONTINUOUS

Kathy rejoins the girls, who are coming out of the pavilion, and make an outraged fuss over her.

LAURA

Are you all right, Kath?

RUTH

I can't believe he hit you!

KATHY

I don't think he meant to.

RUTH

Are you bleeding?

KATHY

No.

RUTH

He's an animal. That's what I think.

Kathy doesn't respond, and instead looks back to the playing field.

Where she sees Tommy –

– standing on the edge of the playing field, talking to the new Guardian, Miss Lucy.

Tommy and Miss Lucy are too distant for us to hear their conversation, but we can read some of the body language, when Miss Lucy reaches out and touches him lightly on the shoulder.

Whatever Miss Lucy is saying, Tommy is listening intently.

RUTH

A mad animal.

INT. CORRIDOR – DAY

Children are lined to enter the Matron's office for a medical examination.

They are neatly lined, but chatting and unconcerned. These examinations are completely routine.

At the head of the queue are Kathy, Ruth and Amanda.

A group of three children exit Matron's office, followed by Matron herself.

MATRON

Next.

INT. MATRON'S OFFICE – CONTINUOUS

Kathy, Ruth and Amanda are being examined by the Matron, and two male Doctors.

The presence of the two Doctors, and some high-tech pieces of medical equipment, feel unnatural.

One of the Doctors is listening to Ruth's chest with a stethoscope.

Amanda stands in front of the second Doctor, with her arms raised. The man is using his hands to feel around her bare torso, as if looking for lump-tumours or sensitivities.

Matron is examining Kathy, making notes on a clipboard headed: KATHY H.

She tilts Kathy's head to the side, frowning slightly at the slight bruise from where Tommy accidentally struck her.

MATRON

What's this from?

KATHY

(*shrugs*)

Don't remember.

MATRON

Doctor.

The first Doctor glances round from Ruth.

He peers at Kathy's bruise critically. For a beat or two longer than would seem appropriate for such a small contusion.

DOCTOR

It's nothing. Just a bump.

INT. ART ROOM – DAY

A group of the Hailsham students are in the art room, quietly working on paintings and sculptures.

In the corner of the room, another of their Guardians, Miss Geraldine, is helping two of the children mix paint colours.

At her table, Kathy works on a sculpture.

Meanwhile, Ruth pointedly leans over to the table beside them, where Tommy is working.

RUTH

Tommy. What are you doing? Show us so we can have a look.

KATHY

(*quietly, to Ruth*)

No, Ruth. Don't.

Tommy looks up from his drawing, and sees a semicircle of faces looking back at him.

A beat, as he returns their gaze.

Then he spins the picture round so that it faces them.

RUTH

Oh! It's a – (*She feigns uncertainty.*) What is it exactly?

AMANDA

I think it must be a dog. Is it a dog, Tommy?

One of the boys, Arthur – who had been one of the team-pickers from the playing fields – joins in.

ARTHUR

It can't be a dog. Its eyes are too small. I think it must be a kind of rat.

AMANDA

Yes! That's it! Tommy's drawn a rat. Ruth, do you think Tommy's rat will be selected for the Gallery?

RUTH

I don't know. Why don't we ask Miss Geraldine to come over and tell us what she thinks?

Close-up on Tommy's face – flushing.

TOMMY

It's not finished yet.

ARTHUR

That's right. You need to draw the whiskers.

TOMMY

It's not a rat.

AMANDA

And a longer tail.

TOMMY

(*voice rising*)

It's not a rat!

On the other side of the room, the raised voice makes Miss Geraldine's head turn.

RUTH
(*whispers*)

Here it comes!

The kids goading Tommy wait expectantly.

Then Tommy speaks.

And the calmness has returned to his voice.

TOMMY

It's not a rat. (*Beat.*) It's an elephant.

He spins the picture back to face him, and continues to work on it.

Ruth and Amanda exchange a slightly puzzled glance –

– but let it go, because Miss Geraldine is now walking over to their table –

– and the kids return to their respective works.

INT. MISS LUCY'S STUDY – DAY

In her small study, Miss Lucy is writing at her desk.

Kathy appears in the doorway.

Miss Lucy seems unaware.

KATHY

Miss Lucy.

Miss Lucy looks up.

Then smiles.

MISS LUCY

Hello.

KATHY

Kathy. Kathy H.

MISS LUCY

Yes, of course. Kathy H. Come in.

Kathy takes a step into Miss Lucy's office.

MISS LUCY

What can I do for you?

KATHY

I was wondering what you said to Tommy.

Miss Lucy doesn't seem to follow. Perhaps having to remember exactly who Tommy is.

MISS LUCY

I'm sorry?

KATHY

You said something to Tommy. Out on the playing fields. And whatever it was, it's had quite an effect on him.

MISS LUCY

I see.

Bemused, but seeing the seriousness in Kathy's face, Miss Lucy makes an effort to be precise.

MISS LUCY

So – what was it I said? I believe I was trying to calm him down, because he seemed so upset. And he explained that he was often teased about things like sport, and art. So I told him that he shouldn't get upset at these things. The other children are only teasing him to get a reaction. (*Beat.*) And if it happens that he isn't particularly good at sport or art, well – it doesn't matter. It's not so important.

Kathy frowns.

KATHY

Not so important.

Miss Lucy shrugs, almost as if to shrug off the intense gaze of the little girl in front of her.

MISS LUCY

No. Not really.

INT. REFECTORY – DAY

Lunch, in Hailsham's refectory.

Trays contain compartments filled with extremely overcooked food. Grey meat and faded vegetables.

The kids take the trays from the food trolleys, then take seats at long refectory tables.

Kathy is carrying her tray with Ruth, Amanda and Laura.

She sees Tommy.

As the other girls move forward with their trays . . .

. . . Kathy hangs back.

INT. REFECTORY – DAY

Tommy sits at a table with a few spaces around him.

We can sense he is used to eating alone.

Not least from the surprise in his face when he looks up, and sees Kathy taking the seat opposite him.

TOMMY

Kathy. (*Awkward.*) Aren't you sitting with the girls?

Kathy looks around, as if half expecting to find the girls either side of her.

Then she looks back at Tommy.

KATHY

I just checked, and I'm pretty sure I'm not sitting with the girls. I'm sitting with you.

Tommy smiles.

TOMMY

I wanted to say I was sorry. I didn't mean to hit you when – (*He breaks off.*) I mean, I wouldn't want to hit any girl. But particularly not you.

KATHY

Well. It was an accident, that's all.

A passing Guardian, Miss Geraldine, glances at Tommy's plate.

At the collection of over-boiled carrots, not eaten as yet.

MISS GERALDINE

Tommy. Finish those vegetables.

Miss Geraldine moves on.

Kathy leaves a calculated pause.

KATHY

So . . . you didn't lose your temper when they were teasing you earlier. In the art room.

Tommy looks around.

At this moment, the seats immediately beside Tommy and Kathy are taken by some kids coming over with their trays.

About to reply, Tommy seems to think the better of it – apparently uncomfortable about their conversation being overheard.

TOMMY

Why don't we talk about it at the pond?

EXT. POND – DAY

At the back of Hailsham, tucked away in the grounds, is a large pond surrounded by bulrushes and overhanging trees.

Hailsham is reflected in the water.

It's quiet. Feels private.

Tommy sits on a large flat rock, with Kathy beside him.

TOMMY

I'm not going to get angry like that any more.

KATHY

Because of what Miss Lucy told you? About being creative.

TOMMY

How do you know about that?

KATHY

I'm nosy. (*Beat.*) She can't actually mean that being creative isn't important, can she? What about the Gallery? If being creative isn't important, why have a gallery at all?

TOMMY

I don't know. (*Beat.*) I think this shouldn't be spread, okay? It's not the kind of thing that should get around, because Miss Lucy is a new guardian.

KATHY

Yes.

From the litter and detritus collected at the edge of the pond, cut to:

INT. THEATRE – DAY

A scene from an anonymous film. Black and white, from the thirties, forties or fifties. The scene is a caperish moment of chase, or slapstick –

– which is being watched, with delight, by Kathy, Tommy, Ruth, Arthur, Laura, and all other students in their year.

As the moment of slapstick resolves, the kids all shout:

STUDENTS

Again, again!

The scene is rewound, and begins again.

INT. CORRIDOR – DAY

We follow Miss Geraldine down a corridor.

Miss Geraldine is carrying a large stack of papers – drawings and paintings by the students from the art room.

INT. OUTSIDE BILLIARD ROOM – CONTINUOUS

Miss Geraldine carries the artworks into the billiard room, where we glimpse Miss Emily and two other Guardians.

One of the Guardians closes the door behind Miss Geraldine . . .

. . . on Kathy and Ruth, who are in the corridor outside.

INT. HAILSHAM – CONTINUOUS

We now follow Kathy and Ruth as they run through the school.

INT. HAILSHAM/BACK DOOR – CONTINUOUS

As they run out of the back door, they hold out their wrists to swipe their metal bracelets against a featureless metal box, attached to the wall.

The metal box gives an electronic bleep in acknowledgment.

EXT. HAILSHAM – CONTINUOUS

Kathy and Ruth continue running, heading round the side of the building . . .

. . . then up on to a low flower-bed wall, which allows them to peer through the window of the billiard room.

Where they can see Miss Emily, Miss Geraldine, and two other Guardians.

They are laying out paintings, drawings and sculptures on tables and easels.

Through the glass, we can faintly hear Miss Emily.

MISS EMILY

Put these two together. Yes . . . perfect. I think she'll find this one very interesting.

RUTH

(*quiet, to Kathy*)

Madame is coming.

EXT. HAILSHAM – NIGHT

A constellation in the night sky above Hailsham.

INT. GIRLS' DORMITORY – NIGHT

Rows of beds in the girls' dormitory.

Beside each bed, a bedside table. And on each bedside table, a collection.

Kathy's collection mainly consists of books, and Ruth's collection is of model horses.

Kathy is lying in her bed, looking at the ceiling.

Thinking.

After a couple of moments, she looks to her side.

In the next bed is Ruth, whose eyes are closed.

KATHY

Ruth.

No response.

KATHY

Ruth. Are you awake?

RUTH

No. I'm asleep. And this is the dream I'm having.

KATHY

Why do you think Madame comes and takes our artwork? What's it for exactly?

Ruth's eyes open.

RUTH

It's for the Gallery.

Kathy rolls over, to face Ruth.

KATHY

But that's what I mean. She comes here – what, twice a year – and selects our best pictures and sculptures and poems. And takes them away.

RUTH

Maybe she sells them. Outside, out there, they sell everything.

KATHY

Maybe.

A moment of silence, as both Kathy and Ruth contemplate these thoughts.

Then:

RUTH

She's scared of us.

Kathy frowns, and props herself up in bed.

KATHY

Madame?

RUTH

Yes.

KATHY

That's a strange thing to say.

Ruth shrugs.

RUTH

I used to think she was just snooty, but now I know different.

KATHY

I don't understand. How could Madame be scared of us? What could we do to her?

RUTH

I don't know. I don't think we could do anything. But I've been remembering her last visit.

KATHY

And?

RUTH

I don't know. Little things. The way she looks at us.

Beat.

RUTH

She's scared all right. (*Beat.*) I bet I could prove it.

KATHY

. . . How?

EXT. HAILSHAM – DAY

We watch as, from a distance, a lone car approaches Hailsham along a ribbon of road through the surrounding fields.

INT. WINDOW – DAY

Kathy, Ruth, Amanda, Laura and the five other girls stand in the shadows of Hailsham's front doorway, watching the car approach.

EXT. DRIVEWAY – DAY

The car pulls up on the gravel courtyard of Hailsham, and parks.

The driver, Madame, exits the car, then goes around to the boot –

– which she opens.

Inside is her luggage – a small overnight bag. She takes it out, closes the boot, then turns –

– and starts.

Because surrounding her, in a tight circle, are the nine girls.

There are standing several feet away, not moving. Just looking at Madame.

A beat. Frozen and uncertain for Madame.

Then she starts to walk.

And almost as soon as she does so –

– the children start to walk too.

Moving straight for her. Making her stop again in her tracks, and hold the overnight bag to her chest.

In a slightly stiff, glazed way, the girls each murmur, dream-like –

GIRLS

Excuse me, miss.

– as they pass her.

Then they separate, each walking in different directions . . .

. . . leaving Madame alone.

It's a very odd moment. Surreal. But it reveals exactly what Ruth said it would.

Madame's reaction was as if she were suppressing a shudder. A kind of dread in her eyes, looking at the children as if they were spiders.

As if she were afraid they might reach out and touch her.

EXT. HAILSHAM – DAY

Around the side of the building, the girls reconvene.

One of the girls, Laura, looks particularly shaken and close to tears.

RUTH

You saw it, didn't you? In her face. You all saw it.

AMANDA

Yes.

RUTH

There's no doubt. Kathy?

KATHY

(*confirms*)

No doubt.

LAURA

If she doesn't like us, why does she want our artwork? Why doesn't she just leave us alone?

The response from the others is silence.

There seems to be no answer to these questions.

INT. GIRLS' DORM – DAY

Kathy is alone, gazing at herself in a wall-length mirror. Over this, we start to hear the Hailsham school song.

INT. ASSEMBLY HALL – DAY

The school song leads us to the main hall, where it is being sung by the students of Hailsham, standing in rows for morning assembly. There are about eighty of them, of ages ranging from five to eighteen.

Two younger children are whispering until they are silenced by a frown from the head Guardian, Miss Emily.

When the song has finished, Miss Emily prepares to address them from a lectern on a raised stage.

Behind her, the other Guardians stand. Among them is Madame.

MISS EMILY

Good morning, students.

STUDENTS

Good morning, Miss Emily.

MISS EMILY

There are several points of order. The first is that Madame Marie-Claude is visiting us today, and will be examining your works.

Miss Emily turns to acknowledge Madame, who nods in reply.

MISS EMILY

We will of course extend her every courtesy, and make her feel most welcome.

Kathy and Ruth exchange a glance.

MISS EMILY

Second point of order. It has come to my attention that three burned cigarettes were discovered, hidden behind a pot in the flower garden.

Miss Geraldine holds up a glass jam jar, containing the offending cigarette butts.

MISS EMILY

I know that on occasion students have seen some of the caretakers or delivery men smoking cigarettes. But I must emphasise, once again, that it is much, much worse for a student of Hailsham to smoke than anyone else. I should not have to explain that students of Hailsham are special. Keeping yourselves well, keeping yourselves healthy inside, is of paramount importance. Have I made myself clear?

STUDENTS

Yes, Miss Emily.

MISS EMILY

Good. (*Beat.*) And finally, I have a piece of good news for all students who have been diligent in collecting tokens. At the end of studies tomorrow, there will be a sale.

This piece of news creates an immediate buzz of excitement in the students –

– quietened by Miss Emily raising a hand.

MISS EMILY

The delivery will arrive in the morning. And I was assured by the van driver that the boxes would contain . . .

Miss Emily pauses deliberately, raising the students' expectations.

She extends the pause, then allows a slight smile to creep into the corner of her mouth.

MISS EMILY

. . . a bumper crop.

The assembly hall erupts with the students' cheers.

INT. THEATRE – LATER

Five students appear to be rehearsing a play, watched by Miss Lucy. Among the students on the stage are Kathy, Tommy and Laura.

Watching from the seats are the rest of Kathy's year, including Ruth and Amanda.

There are a few props on the stage. A table, trays, plates. All other objects in the rehearsal – cash register, milk, sugar – are mimed.

Kathy is on one side of the table, playing the roll of a cashier, and the others are queuing for the till.

Laura is first in line. Tommy is behind her.

KATHY

Good morning, ma'am.

LAURA

Good morning.

KATHY

Can I help you?

LAURA

I wanted two teas. Milk in one tea, and milk and sugar in the other.

KATHY

Two teas. Right.

Kathy turns behind her and mimes pouring milk into two mugs. Then she hands the non-existent mugs to Laura.

LAURA

You forgot the sugar.

The students in the seats laugh.

Kathy rolls her eyes, and mimes adding sugar.

Laura moves on.

Tommy, behind Laura, misses his cue to move forwards.

Miss Lucy prompts him.

MISS LUCY

Tommy.

Tommy snaps to focus, steps forwards and blurts:

TOMMY

Two teas. Milk in one, and milk and sugar in the other.

MISS LUCY

No, Tommy. I want to hear your own order. Don't simply repeat the one you just heard.

Tommy looks back blankly at Miss Lucy.

MISS LUCY

What other kind of drinks do they serve in cafés?

Pause.

TOMMY

Water?

Some of the kids in the audience laugh.

Ruth heckles from the front row.

RUTH

A drink you pay for, you oaf.

KATHY
(*whispers*)

Coffee.

TOMMY
(*to Miss Lucy*)

Coffee.

MISS LUCY

So then.

Tommy shoots Kathy a grateful smile.

TOMMY
(*to Kathy*)

Two coffees. Milk in one, and milk and sugar in the other.

As Kathy mimes the drinks:

MISS EMILY
(*out of shot*)

Once lubrication is established, the penis is inserted thus.

Cut to:

INT. CLASSROOM – DAY

A skeleton, lying on a desk, with legs spread.

A long wooden ruler is inserted between the legs, into what would be the vaginal opening to the hip bone cavity.

The ruler is being held by Miss Emily.

MISS EMILY

The appropriate friction between penis and vagina should result in orgasm for both parties.

Watching Miss Emily, fascinated, but not convulsed in either amusement or embarrassment, is Kathy's class.

MISS EMILY

What constitutes appropriate friction will vary according to the physiology of the sexual partners.

Miss Emily uses her hand to raise the skeleton's hips.

MISS EMILY

Here, I am illustrating how – by arching her back, or perhaps with the aid of a pillow – the woman can arrange herself to create the precise kind of friction she requires.

Miss Emily releases the skeleton's hips and turns to the class.

MISS EMILY

The various positions and pleasures of intercourse must not blind you, however, to its inherent dangers. You are already aware of sexually transmitted diseases, which can wreak havoc on otherwise perfectly healthy bodies.

Miss Emily pauses a moment, distracted by a stray thought pattern.

Then:

MISS EMILY

But some dangers are more complex and insidious. Sex affects the emotions in ways you can never expect. And we can't legislate for that which we do not expect. (*Beat.*) Unavoidably, such emotions remain out of our full control.

Cut to:

EXT. PLAYING FIELDS – DAY

Arthur swinging a rounders bat, and connecting with the ball, which has been pitched by Kathy.

The ball arcs high up into the air, towards the outfield . . .

. . . where Tommy is fielding.

KATHY

Catch it, Tommy!

Tommy tracks the ball, walking backwards, looking for the catch.

As it drops down, he reaches for it.

And misses it.

The ball flies over his head, bounces as it hits the ground, and bounces on towards the far perimeter of the playing field . . .

. . . where it passes a wire fence, only waist high, and comes to rest in the long grass, two or three metres further on.

Tommy approaches the boundary fence. He sees the ball, but makes no attempt to reach it.

Cut to:

Miss Lucy, standing with the batting team.

The batting team are watching Arthur's victory lap, cheering.

But Miss Lucy, her expression unreadable, is watching Tommy . . .

. . . who now turns from the ball, and starts jogging back to the game.

INT. GIRLS' CHANGING ROOM – CONTINUOUS

Miss Lucy is watching the girls getting changed from their whites.

After a couple of moments, she glances out of the changing room, where, down the corridor, she can see the female Guardian – who seems to be in conversation with a boy who is out of our line of sight.

Miss Lucy looks back to the girls. Then, with a discreetly enforced casualness, asks:

MISS LUCY

Why didn't Tommy get the ball?

Ruth and Kathy, who are closest to her, look up.

Kathy notices that Miss Lucy's hands are trembling.

RUTH

Excuse me, Miss Lucy?

MISS LUCY

Why didn't Tommy get the ball? When it bounced over the fence. It couldn't have been far from him.

The other girls have now tuned in to this exchange, and all look at Miss Lucy, confused.

KATHY

The fence is the boundary of the Hailsham grounds.

RUTH

Why take the risk?

MISS LUCY

. . . What risk?

LAURA

We don't go outside the boundary, Miss Lucy. It's too dangerous.

MISS LUCY

Dangerous.

RUTH

There was once a boy who had a big row with all his friends, and ran off beyond the boundaries. And they found him two days later in the woods, tied to a tree.

AMANDA

With his hands and feet cut off.

LAURA

Dead.

Miss Lucy looks shocked.

MISS LUCY

And when was this supposed to have happened?

LAURA

It was before we all got here.

AMANDA

But only just before.

RUTH

And there was the girl who climbed over the fence by the front gate.

MISS LUCY

What happened to her?

RUTH

She climbed over to see what it was like outside.

LAURA

This was in the older days, when the guardians were much stricter. Before Miss Emily.

RUTH

And when she tried to get back, she wasn't allowed. But she kept hanging around outside, pleading, and they still wouldn't let her in. And then she starved out there, right by the gates.

Beat.

MISS LUCY

Who told you these stories?

RUTH

Everybody knows them.

MISS LUCY

And how do you know they're true?

Ruth shrugs.

RUTH

Of course they're true.

Ruth glances to Kathy, as if for confirmation.

Kathy is tying up her shoelaces.

RUTH

Who'd make up stories as horrible as that?

INT. GIRLS' DORMITORY – NIGHT

Kathy's face.

Reveal she's in her bed.

Ruth and Kathy are the only girls awake.

They are moonlit.

Kathy lies on her back, gazing at the ceiling.

Ruth lies on her side, gazing at Kathy.

RUTH

Have you heard the rumour? (*Beat.*) There's a rumour going round. Started by some of the older kids. Something about boyfriends and girlfriends. Apparently they can get preferential treatment when they leave Hailsham.

KATHY

What sort of preferential treatment?

RUTH

I don't know. Just that it's something to do with couples.

KATHY

There are always stories going round. Like the stories about kids who leave the boundary. It was obvious Miss Lucy didn't believe that for a minute.

Beat.

RUTH

I think Laura likes Arthur.

KATHY

All the girls like Arthur, don't they?

RUTH

Maybe. (*Beat.*) I'm not sure you do,

KATHY

He's not my type.

A loaded beat.

Then:

RUTH

Tommy's changed.

KATHY

Changed how?

RUTH

Just changed. That's all.

A moment of silence.

RUTH

I think Laura and Arthur will be the first in our year to have sex, because if Arthur wanted to, Laura wouldn't stop him.

KATHY

I'm sure you're right.

RUTH

Right about Laura wouldn't stop him, or right about them being the first to have sex?

Kathy rolls over on her side, and closes her eyes.

KATHY

Both, I'm sure.

Ruth stays in the same position, eyes remaining open, watching Kathy.

EXT. FOREST – DAY

Kathy is tied to a tree. Her hands and feet have been cut off.

Cut to:

INT. GIRLS' DORMITORY – NIGHT

Kathy's eyes flick open. Waking from her dream.

EXT. OUTSIDE GIRLS' DORMITORY – MORNING

In the corridor outside the girl's dormitory, a long table holds a line of milk-filled glasses.

Beside each glass is a small pill cup.

A Guardian is moving down the table, putting three pills in each cup.

Behind, a line of Girls wait to take their morning cocktail of medication.

EXT. HAILSHAM – MORNING

By the front entrance, a delivery truck has pulled up on the gravel driveway.

From the back, two Delivery Men in overalls are unloading boxes.

Various kids are watching them, intensely curious, but keeping an appropriate distance.

Among the kids are Kathy, Ruth and Tommy.

One of the younger kids, a Girl about eight or nine years old, calls to one of the Delivery Men:

GIRL

Is it really a bumper crop?

One of the Delivery Men looks round. Sees the kids faces.

DELIVERY MAN

I'd say so, sweetheart. A bumper crop.

INT. HAILSHAM – DAY

A school bell is ringing.

Over the ringing, we can hear excited shouts, and laughter.

INT. SCHOOL CORRIDOR – CONTINUOUS

We pick up Kathy running down a corridor in Hailsham –

– being tugged along by Ruth's hand.

And we see that they are at the head of a large group of children, who are also running . . .

. . . and being joined by other children, streaming out of classrooms and side corridors.

Tommy is ahead of them.

We lose Kathy and Ruth and Tommy in the mass of kids . . .

. . . and track the mass of children through the school.

Out of the corridor . . .

Up the stairs . . .

Along another corridor . . .

Until they explode into the –

INT. SALE ROOM – CONTINUOUS

Sale room, where the sale is now under way.

The refectory tables double as stalls, with the sale items laid out along them.

The oldest children work as monitors, standing behind the tables, exchanging tokens for goods, and keeping their highly excited young customers under control.

We track along one refectory table, seeing the excited faces and grabbing hands of the kids on the other side, as they pick up the sale items, searching for the best stuff at the best prices.

And we finally see the sale items themselves –

– which reveal themselves to be the kind of things one might find in a junk shop, or a car-boot sale.

Nothing new, nothing complete. Toys out of the their boxes. Watches with no clasp on the strap. The top half of a tracksuit. Football boots without laces.

Among the kids, we see the faces of children we have already met, including Ruth, Tommy, Arthur, Laura and Amanda.

We pick up Tommy, who has found something, but we can't see what it is.

He pays a Guardian in tokens.

To the side, another Guardian notes down on a clipboard what the kids are purchasing.

INT. SALE ROOM – CONTINUOUS

We pick up Kathy at the back of the throng, gazing at Miss Lucy.

There is a frozen quality to Miss Lucy's expression.

Miss Lucy is seeing what we are seeing – that the objects of the children's enthusiasm are worthless.

In front of Miss Lucy, we catch two of the children having a slightly giddy exchange. Arthur has found a book – Acting Techniques of the Stage and Screen.

ARTHUR

Acting Techniques of the Stage and Screen. It's all the tricks of the trade.

LAURA

It's perfect! Everyone knows you're a natural for acting.

ARTHUR

If I was really serious about it, I'd have to go to America to have the best chance.

Kathy watches Miss Lucy for a moment. Hearing the conversation.

Then turns, and starts moving away from the tables, not towards them.

INT. CORRIDOR – CONTINUOUS

Kathy sits in the corridor outside the saleroom, where chairs have been stacked to clear the space.

She chooses one, and sits.

A moment.

Then:

TOMMY

Hey.

Kathy turns, and sees Tommy beside her.

TOMMY

Aren't you buying? If you've already spent all your tokens, you can have some of mine . . .

KATHY

I have tokens. (*Beat.*) I'll wait until the rush has died down a bit. I'm sure something good will be left.

Beat.

TOMMY

What's the matter, Kath? Ever since our conversation the other day, you've been a bit out of sorts.

Kathy considers this a moment.

And her gaze catches sight of Miss Lucy talking to Miss Geraldine on the other side of the hall.

A short silence.

TOMMY

Well, anyway. It doesn't matter if you can't find anything in the sale –

Tommy reaches into his pocket.

TOMMY

– because I already found something for you.

He produces a cassette tape.

On the cover, it reads: 'Songs After Dark, by Judy Bridgewater'. The cover shows a woman, presumably the singer, wearing an off-the-shoulder purple satin dress. There are palm trees behind her, and a black waiter in a white tuxedo is bringing her a drink.

A cigarette burns in her hand.

Cut to:

Kathy's response. Genuine surprise and delight.

KATHY

A music tape?

TOMMY

I don't know much about it. If it's much good or anything.

Kathy leans forwards and gives Tommy a kiss on the cheek.

KATHY

Thank you!

From the expression on Tommy's face, this was clearly worth the tokens.

INT. GIRLS' DORMITORY – SUNSET

Kathy is alone in the girls' dormitory.

Outside the window, the light is a deep yellow from sunset, and it bathes the room.

Dust motes hang in light shafts.

Kathy has the tape that Tommy gave her, and she is inserting it into a cassette player shared by the girls in that room.

She presses 'Play' –

– and a song starts.

It's a slow ballad. The singer, Judy Bridgewater, is American.

Kathy is immediately transported by the sound.

She reacts as if it is the saddest, most beautiful song she has ever heard.

As the song moves into its second verse, Kathy picks up a small pillow from one of the beds, and holds it close to her chest, as she starts to sway in time to the music.

By the time the second chorus comes around, she has learned the melody, and picked up the repeating lyric of the chorus: 'Baby, never let me go.'

Her eyes close, and she starts to mouth these words . . .

. . . until the short song is over.

As the noise from the cassette player returns to the hiss between music tracks, Kathy opens her eyes, as if waking from a dream –

– to find herself looking at Madame, framed in the doorway of the dormitory.

Both Kathy and Madame are frozen in the act of seeing each other.

But whereas Kathy's expression is simple surprise, Madame has tears pouring down her face.

In fact, she is sobbing.

A beat later, Madame turns, quickly, and leaves.

And her hurried footsteps disappear down the corridor.

EXT. HAILSHAM – DAY. RAIN

The next day.

Rain falls from a slate sky.

EXT. POND – CONTINUOUS

A low mist of exploding water droplets lies over the pond surface.

EXT. WINDOW – CONTINUOUS

Miss Lucy looks at the rain out of a half-open window.

INT. CLASSROOM – CONTINUOUS

Rain blows through the half-open window.

It collects on the interior windowsill and drips onto the floor.

Behind Miss Lucy, a map of the UK is pulled down over the blackboard.

It shudders in the wind.

Reveal Miss Lucy's class. Kathy, Ruth, Tommy, Arthur, Laura, Amanda, and the others of that year. All seated at their desks.

There is an odd electricity in the air. The children don't know what Miss Lucy is about to say. But they sense it is seismic. So they sit, and wait.

Until she speaks.

MISS LUCY

I don't think I can keep silent any more. If no one else will talk to you, I will.

The wind from the open window blows a couple of papers off her desk.

As they drift to the floor, Tommy, in the front row, makes a move to pick them up.

MISS LUCY

No, Tommy – please. I just want you all to listen.

Tommy slides back into his seat.

MISS LUCY

The problem is that you have been told, and not told. That is what I've seen while I've been here. You have been told, but none of you really understand. So I've decided I'll talk to you in a way that you will understand.

Beat.

MISS LUCY

Do you know what happens to children when they grow up?

Silence.

MISS LUCY

No – you don't. Because nobody knows.

On Arthur.

MISS LUCY

They might grow up to become actors, and move to America. Or they might work in supermarkets, or teach in schools. They might become sportsmen, or bus conductors, or racing-car drivers. They might do almost anything.

(*Beat.*) But with you, we do know. None of you will go to America. None of you will work in supermarkets. None of you will do anything, except live out the life that has already been set out for you. (*Beat.*) You will become adults, but only briefly. Before you are old, before you are even middle-aged, you will start to donate your vital organs. That's what you were created to do. And some time around your third or fourth donation, your short life will be complete.

Miss Lucy turns back to the window.

MISS LUCY

You have to know who you are, and what you are. It's the only way you'll lead decent lives.

End on the reaction of the kids.

Stunned. Not certain what to say, or do. Except remain locked to their seats, and wait for the moment to go away.

Apart from Tommy, who now reaches down, picks up the fallen papers, and hands them to Miss Lucy.

Cut to:

EXT. HAILSHAM – DAY

The view across the grounds to the school.

KATHY

(*voice-over*)

It surprises me to think that Miss Lucy was only actually with us at Hailsham for a few weeks. Not really very long at all. (*Beat.*) Yet by the time she left, everything was different somehow.

INT. ASSEMBLY HALL – DAY

The Hailsham students stand in the assembly hall.

Ruth and Tommy are standing beside each other.

Kathy is one row back.

Miss Emily addresses the students from the lectern.

MISS EMILY

I have only one announcement this morning, which is to say that Miss Lucy, who was guardian to the fourth-year students, is no longer working at Hailsham.

A shocked ripple response from the ranks of the standing children.

Noticeably from Tommy.

MISS EMILY

A replacement will be found for her, but in the meantime her classes will be divided between Miss Geraldine and myself.

She pauses.

MISS EMILY

It is hard, is it not, to continue in the face of deliberate subversion. There are those who would seek to thwart us. This is clear.

Miss Emily closes her eyes. Talks now to an interior voice, losing track of the faces before her.

MISS EMILY

And we are aware that the tide is not with forward thinking. It never is. No – the tide is with the entrenched mindset. With values that are unexamined. (*Beat.*) But I will not be coerced.

Silence.

Which now extends.

As it does so, cut to:

A girl's hand, tentatively slipping into a boy's hand.

After a moment's hesitation, the boy's fingers close around the girl's.

Reveal it is Ruth and Tommy, and we are seeing from Kathy's point of view.

Cut back to:

Miss Emily's eyes, as they flick open.

Relocating her. Reminding her of the audience.

MISS EMILY

I will not be coerced!

The barked words echo faintly in the hall.

MISS EMILY

No! *And neither will Hallsham!*

Sensing a cue, the collected children and Guardians all break into applause.

All except Kathy.

She is reverberating with what she has just seen pass between Ruth and Tommy.

EXT. PATH – DAY

Kathy walks down a path through trees at the back of Hailsham, towards –

EXT. POND – CONTINUOUS

The pond.

Across the water is the large flat rock.

On which Ruth and Tommy are sitting.

Chatting. Unaware of Kathy's presence on the far side of the pond.

KATHY

(*voice-over*)

I didn't understand why, after all her teasing, Ruth would decide that Tommy was the boy she liked most of all.

Kathy watches as Ruth turns Tommy's face towards hers.

KATHY
(*voice-over*)

They say girls are always mean to the boys they like. So maybe Ruth had liked him all along.

Kathy stops, as –

– Ruth leans forwards to kiss Tommy.

Back to Kathy's face, frozen.

KATHY
(*voice-over*)

Maybe I should have teased him too.

INT. GIRLS' DORMITORY

Kathy's collection sits on her bedside table.

The small row of books.

A fountain pen.

And the Judy Bridgewater cassette.

She puts another book into her collection.

INT. GIRLS' DORMITORY

The collection grows.

Reveal Kathy, now in her late teens, packing a bag.

EXT. HAILSHAM

The view across the pond.

The school building is reflected in the water.

Then splintered into ripples.

On this splintered image –

Fade to black.

PART 2: THE COTTAGES

Fade up to:

INT. MINIBUS

A minibus drives through flat countryside.

The bus is being driven by a man in his early sixties – Keffers.

In the back are six Hailsham students, now aged eighteen.

Among them, Kathy, Ruth and Tommy.

Kathy and Tommy we have seen before in adult incarnation, at the start of the film. Ruth we recognise by the colour of her hair . . .

. . . and by the way her hand is enmeshed in Tommy's.

All are glazed by the length of the journey.

Gazing out of the window, watching the largely featureless landscape slide by.

KATHY
(*voice-over*)
We left Hailsham at eighteen.

EXT. DIRT ROAD – DAY

The minibus drives up a long dirt road.

KATHY
(*voice-over*)
My year were scattered to different locations, but Tommy, Ruth and I were relocated together, to a collection of buildings that had once been a working farm.

At the far end of the dirt road, a cluster of farm buildings can be seen.

KATHY
(*voice-over*)
We called them the Cottages.

EXT. THE COTTAGES – DAY

A small collection of farm buildings, with a central house, are nestled in remote countryside.

But it is not picturesque. It is desolate. Old farm machinery lies where it was last used. A couple of chickens run through the muddy space between the buildings.

KATHY
(*voice-over*)
At the time, we thought the Cottages were just a staging post before the donation centres.

A minibus pulls up outside, and the students get out, each carrying a rucksack and a suitcase.

They all look slightly taken aback by what they see.

Keffers directs them unceremoniously to the main house.

KATHY
(*voice-over*)
But looking back, I can see they were actually a training ground of sorts. During our time there, some of us would be expected to volunteer as carers.

As the students walk to the house, they have to pick their way across the mud. Their shoes are unsuitable. Their clothing looks insufficient for the cold.

Standing in the doorway of the main house is a girl. Slightly older. She wears a heavy jumper and wellington boots. This is Chrissie.

Chrissie watches them blankly as they approach.

KATHY
(*voice-over*)
The Cottages were also our first contact with those who had not had the privilege of growing up in Hailsham.

Fade in the sound of a TV sitcom laughter track.

Cut to:

INT. LIVING ROOM – NIGHT

In the living room are Ruth and Tommy. They are sitting on a sofa. Ruth is leaning back into Tommy's arms.

At the other end of the sofa is Kathy.

On another sofa is Chrissie.

Entering the room is Rodney, Chrissie's boyfriend.

As he walks behind Chrissie, he gives her shoulder a little squeeze. Then sits beside her, and she slips her arm into his. As a gesture, it is clingy. As a rule, whenever Rodney and Chrissie are near each other, they hold each other in such a way.

All of them have slightly glazed expressions –

– because they are watching the TV, which is showing a generic American sitcom, circa early nineties.

In the background, other inhabitants of the Cottages come and go. On the floor are empty plates of food, presumably from a dinner eaten in front of the television.

Close up on the TV screen –

– where a group of attractive young Americans are sitting around in a New York apartment.

One of the Handsome Boys on the TV shakes his head at one of the Pretty Girls.

HANDSOME BOY

Hey Jen, what's this I keep hearing about you and Ricky?

PRETTY GIRL 1

Ricky? I don't know what you're talking about.

PRETTY GIRL 2

Oh – can help you out there. He's talking about blue eyes, blonde hair, cute dimples when he smiles, and biceps that can crack walnuts.

Handsome Boy winces.

HANDSOME BOY

Ouch.

PRETTY GIRL I

Oh, that Ricky.

HANDSOME BOY

Jennifer, get real. I saw you with him.

PRETTY GIRL 2

Jen and Ricky, sitting in a tree, K-I-S-S-I-N-G.

Pretty Girl 1 looks indignant, and rolls her eyes.

PRETTY GIRL I

That is so not true! (*Beat.*) We weren't in a tree.

The laughter track kicks in again.

EXT. COTTAGES – MORNING

Daybreak over the fields around the Cottages.

EXT. COTTAGES – CONTINUOUS

Keffers pulls up in his minibus outside the main house.

He gets out, and picks up a box of groceries from the passenger seat.

As he carries the box across the muddy yard to the main house, he slips.

Keffers breaks his fall by landing on one knee, and he manages to keep the box of groceries upright.

But when he rises, his leg is caked with mud. He looks immensely pissed off.

Kathy is standing in the doorway of the main house to take the box.

KATHY

Thank you, Mr Keffers.

Keffers hands her the box and starts walking back across the yard without saying a word.

INT. KITCHEN – DAY

Kathy, alone, fixes herself a cup of tea, reading a book while the kettle boils.

INT. LANDING – CONTINUOUS

Kathy carries the tea and book up the stairs to her bedroom.

As she walks down the landing, she passes Tommy's room.

The door is slightly ajar. Through the slight gap, she glimpses Ruth and Tommy having sex.

Kathy continues to her room and shuts the door behind her.

INT. KITCHEN – DAY

The same group of people that were watching TV – Kathy, Ruth, Tommy, Rodney and Chrissie – are in the kitchen fixing breakfast.

Chrissie and Ruth are cooking up some scrambled eggs, and the others are sitting at the table.

Also at the table are two other young people. One reads a book, and the other eats cereal while reading the back of the cereal packet.

Kathy is eating cereal too, and has an open book in front of her . . .

. . . but is tuned in to Ruth and Chrissie's conversation.

RUTH

I'm not even saying I'll apply to be a carer. Just several people have told me I'd be good at it. But then Laura went around telling people that I had been saying I was the most likely to get selected.

Chrissie rolls her eyes.

CHRISSIE

That is so not true.

RUTH

(*echoes, in agreement*)

So not true.

Kathy, subtly, reacts.

Ruth brings over a plate of scrambled eggs and puts them in front of Tommy.

As she does so, she gives his shoulder a little squeeze.

INT. KITCHEN – LATER

The kitchen is now empty apart from Kathy and Ruth, who stand at the sink, washing up.

While Kathy washes, Ruth dries.

For a while, they do this in silence.

Then Kathy speaks.

KATHY

Ruth, I've been meaning to ask you. Why do you do that thing – squeezing Tommy's shoulder whenever you pass him?

Ruth looks slightly confused.

RUTH

I'm allowed to touch Tommy, aren't I?

KATHY

It's the way you're touching him. You know what I'm talking about. The way you squeeze his shoulder. (*Beat.*) It's copied from that television show.

RUTH

That's –

KATHY

(*cuts in*)

And please don't tell me, 'That's so not true.'

Ruth shuts her mouth.

KATHY

All that behaviour: it's not what people do, out there, in real life, if that's what you were thinking.

Hold on Ruth's face. She looks angry – but unsure how to fight back.

So she shrugs.

RUTH

So what? It's no big deal. A lot of us do it.

KATHY

What you mean is, Chrissie and Rod do it.

And now the anger on Ruth's face becomes, for a flashed moment, triumph.

Which she quickly shifts into concern.

RUTH

Oh, Kathy. So that's what this is about. It must be awful for you, surrounded by all these couples.

KATHY

(*hotly*)

I never said that. I'm just saying it's daft: you copy what they do, and they copy the TV show.

RUTH

But I'm right, aren't I? And you don't like the fact that Tommy and I are friends with Chrissie and Rod. Whereas you hardly talk to anyone.

KATHY

No, you're not right.

Ruth raises her eyebrows.

RUTH

(*sarcastic*)

'So' not right?

Ruth puts her drying cloth down, and walks out of the kitchen.

Leaving Kathy alone.

EXT. FIELD – DAY

In a field adjacent to the farm buildings a car is driving circles.

Through the windscreen, we can see Chrissie behind the wheel.

Rodney is beside her.

The car stalls as Chrissie grinds the gears viciously. Then it stops.

Chrissie restarts the engine, puts the car in gear –

– and almost immediately lurches, and stalls again.

Chrissie bursts into tears.

Although the intensity of her reaction might simply be her frustration at learning to drive, it feels somehow more than that.

EXT. COTTAGES – DAY

Kathy is standing at the rear of the main farmhouse, holding a full rubbish-sack.

She watches the motionless car in the field for a couple of moments.

It doesn't restart.

Then Kathy continues to the bins.

When she opens the lid to put the rubbish sack inside, she sees, sitting on top of the bag already inside . . .

. . . a slightly crumpled pornographic magazine.

Kathy reacts.

Then looks around, to see if anyone is near or can see her.

INT. BARN – DAY

Daylight filters into what was once an old barn, and is now used as a general storage area.

Judging by the dust and cobwebs, the space doesn't get used much.

Kathy sits with the magazine . . .

. . . flicking through the pictures.

We watch Kathy scan the girls. She pauses on each image for the same amount of time, regardless of the pose of size of the photo. Her focus is their faces.

Kathy is absorbed in what she is doing . . .

. . . apparently oblivious to the fact that someone else has entered the barn, and has been watching her.

Until:

KATHY

Hello, Tommy.

Tommy smiles, a little sheepishly.

TOMMY

Hello, Kath.

KATHY

Don't just hover in the doorway. Come in. Join the fun.

Tommy walks over to where Kathy sits.

TOMMY

I didn't know you liked that sort of stuff.

KATHY

Girls are allowed to look too, aren't we?

Beat.

Kathy starts flicking through the pages again.

TOMMY

I wasn't trying to spy on you.

KATHY

You're welcome to take them after I've finished.

Tommy gives a short laugh.

TOMMY

I expect I've seen them all already.

A beat.

Kathy looks up at Tommy again –

– and finds him returning her gaze with a serious expression.

TOMMY

Kath – what are you looking for?

KATHY

What do you mean? I'm just looking at dirty pictures.

TOMMY

Just for kicks?

KATHY

I suppose you could say that.

Tommy sits beside Kathy.

TOMMY

Kath, you don't – (*He breaks off.*) If it's for kicks, you don't do it like that. You have to look at the pictures more carefully. Nothing really happens if you go that fast.

KATHY

How do you know what works for girls?

TOMMY

Kath. You aren't looking for kicks.

A beat.

Kathy stands abruptly, and drops the magazine into Tommy's hands.

KATHY

Here. Give it to Ruth. See if they do anything for her.

She exits.

Tommy watches her go.

INT. KATHY'S ROOM – DAY

Kathy is reading on her bed.

Ruth enters.

RUTH

Hi.

KATHY

Hi.

Ruth sits on the bed.

RUTH

I suppose you've heard what Chrissie and Rod have been saying.

Kathy puts her book down, bristling slightly – thinking that this conversation will relate to their earlier exchange, and that in some way Ruth is going to rub Kathy's nose in her friendship with the older couple.

KATHY

No. I haven't.

RUTH

They're probably just having me on. Their idea of a joke. Forget I mentioned it.

KATHY

You obviously want to tell me.

Beat.

RUTH

You know that Rod and Chrissie have been thinking of applying to be carers. So they've been learning to drive.

KATHY

Yes.

RUTH

Well – last weekend, Rod and Chrissie went for a drive together, and they went up to a town on the Norfolk coast. (*Beat.*) And they think they saw this person.

KATHY

What person?

RUTH

A lady. Working in an open-plan office. And . . .

Ruth glances at Kathy, and suddenly Kathy sees how vulnerable and anxious Ruth looks.

Kathy sits up, concerned, their earlier spat forgotten.

KATHY

What is it, Ruth?

RUTH

I'm sure it's not true. Or a mistake. But – they thought this person was a 'possible'. (*Beat.*) For me.

Kathy looks genuinely amazed.

KATHY

They found your original?

RUTH

They aren't sure, obviously. But Rodney said the resemblance was really striking.

Kathy sits beside Ruth on the bed.

KATHY

My God, Ruth.

RUTH

I know.

KATHY

What are you going to do?

RUTH

Rod and Chrissie want to drive me back up there, so I can see for myself. Tommy will come, but . . . I feel nervous . . .

KATHY

Do you want me to come too?

This is clearly what Ruth was hoping for.

Kathy takes Ruth's hand.

KATHY

Ruth, of course.

EXT. ROAD – DAY

A slightly battered estate car drives along an empty Norfolk A-road.

INT. CAR – CONTINUOUS

Rodney is driving, with Chrissie in the passenger seat.

Kathy, Tommy and Ruth are in the back.

RODNEY

So – exactly how much experience have you guys had with the outside?

RUTH

Quite a lot.

TOMMY

No, we haven't!

RUTH

We did a lot of role-playing exercises in Hailsham.

TOMMY

They don't count.

Rodney and Chrissie exchange a glance.

RODNEY

Okay. Well, don't feel scared. There's really nothing to it.

RUTH

We aren't scared.

RODNEY

Good.

Cut to:

INT. CAFE – DAY

Kathy, Ruth, Tommy, Rodney and Chrissie all sit around a table in a small seaside café for lunch, looking at a menu.

A Waitress is taking their order.

As she waits for them to make up their minds, we see the Waitress reacts slightly to the sight of the bracelets. Not unlike Madame, but perhaps better repressed. A frozen quality in her gaze that betrays the inward shudder.

RODNEY

I'll get sausage, egg and chips.

The Waitress nods and turns to Tommy – who looks slightly panicked, as if confronted with an elaborate menu at an intimidating French restaurant. So he defaults to Rodney's order.

TOMMY

Sausage, egg and chips, please.

RUTH

Yes. Sausage, egg and chips.

KATHY

Sausage, egg, and chips for me too.

Chrissie laughs.

CHRISSIE

I suppose I'd better get the same.

WAITRESS

Right. Five sausage, egg and chips. Drinks?

A beat.

Then Kathy, Ruth and Tommy all look to Rodney.

RODNEY

Five Cokes, please.

INT. CAFE – LATER

The five of them eat their lunch.

The Cokes are circa-1970s bottles of cheap Corona Cola.

Tommy seems distracted by the sight of the sea and the shoreline just outside the window.

They are eating in silence.

Then Chrissie shoots a glance at Rodney, who nods, almost imperceptibly.

Kathy sees it.

CHRISSIE

You know, there's something I've been wanting to talk to you lot about. The problem is that back there, at the Cottages, it's impossible. Someone is always listening in.

Something about Chrissie's tone feels a little over-casual. Again, Kathy notices this – and also the way Rodney has leaned forward, and is now watching Ruth closely.

CHRISSIE

So – it was just something we had heard about Hailsham students. Someone was saying that some Hailsham students, in the past, had managed to get a deferral. Apparently, those Hailsham students could have their first donation put back by three, or even four years. (*Beat.*) As long as they qualified.

Chrissie pauses, and checks the faces of Kathy, Tommy and Ruth, for any clue that they know what she is talking about.

RODNEY

If there was a boy and a girl, and they were in love with each other – really, properly in love, and you could prove it – then you would be given a few years together, before you began your donations.

Tommy is frowning. Clearly, this story is news to him.

RUTH

Where did you hear about this?

RODNEY

When we were at White Mansion.

CHRISSIE

People there used to go on about this Hailsham couple. And when the guy was only a few weeks from donation, he just went to see someone. He applied. And everything got sorted out.

RODNEY

They got three years straight. Three years together, just to themselves. Because they could prove they were properly in love.

Beat.

CHRISSIE

I suppose –

Chrissie can no longer maintain the enforced casualness of her voice.

CHRISSIE

– you lot would know about that. Being from Hailsham. You'd know the rules about that sort of thing.

RODNEY

Who is it you go to? Who would you talk to if you wanted to apply?

Silence.

Until it is broken by Tommy.

TOMMY

To be honest, I don't know what you're talking about.

A flash of anger in Rodney's face.

RODNEY

Oh, come on. Do you expect us to believe that? Everyone knows Hailsham is special. So what is it? Why keep all these things to yourself?

Another silence.

Then Kathy says, delicately:

KATHY

There were lots of stories in Hailsham. I don't think many of them turned out to be true.

EXT. SHORELINE – DAY

Waves lap on a shingle beach. Fade to –

EXT. STREET – CONTINUOUS

And Rodney isn't very sure where he's going.

He turns back to them, talking to no one in particular.

RODNEY

I probably won't be able to find this office again. In fact, I can't even be sure this is the right town.

Ruth is looking quietly desperate.

RUTH

Please do try to remember, Rod.

RODNEY

I'm doing my best. I'm just saying: none of this is looking very familiar.

Kathy walks up to Rodney and speaks quietly but firmly to him.

KATHY

Rod – I hope you didn't make up this possible for Ruth, just to create the opportunity to ask us about Hailsham.

RODNEY

I wasn't making it up.

KATHY

Then I equally hope you are not failing to find the office as a punishment for us not knowing about this deferral scheme.

RODNEY

. . . Of course I'm not.

KATHY

Then find the office. Now.

Rodney nods, clearly a little taken aback by Kathy's tone.

RODNEY

It may have been down here.

EXT. STREET – CONTINUOUS

Kathy, Tommy, Ruth and Chrissie are walking down a street in a seaside down, following Rodney.

EXT. STREET – CONTINUOUS

On Rodney's face.

RODNEY

. . . Yes.

He turns to the others.

RODNEY

Yes. That's it.

The five of them are looking towards an office building, over the road.

The office is glass-fronted, and through the window we can see a large, open-plan room, with a dozen desks arranged in irregular L-patterns.

Some of the office workers are moving between the desks, chatting. Others have pulled their swivel chairs together, and are drinking coffee or eating sandwiches.

The sight of these workers – the sight of these normal lives, unfolding behind the glass – transfixes the five young adults.

KATHY

. . . Do you think it's their lunch break?

TOMMY

It must be . . .

With Kathy, Ruth, Tommy, Rodney and Chrissie, we watch the office workers for a while.

The way their mouths move. Smiling, talking.

The way their eyebrows raise, or the way they shake they heads.

The way they loosen their ties, or roll up their shirtsleeves.

They way they drink their coffee.

We are broken out of the moment by Ruth.

RUTH

(*quietly*)

Oh God. I think I see her.

We see what Ruth sees.

A Woman, about thirty years older than Ruth, in her late forties.

And there is a resemblance there. Facially, and in the way she has tied her hair . . .

. . . but the resemblance is not striking.

RODNEY

Yes. That's her.

But it isn't. This woman is not Ruth's genetic match, with thirty years of age on her. And Kathy knows it.

The five continue watching the Woman for several moments . . .

. . . then one of the other office workers, a Man, notices the five young adults across the road, all staring in at them.

The Man nudges the Woman beside him, and gives a slightly uncertain wave.

This gesture breaks the spell over Kathy, Ruth, Tommy, Rodney and Chrissie . . .

. . . and as one, they all turn and start to walk away.

EXT. SEAFRONT CAR PARK – DAY

Rodney and Chrissie sit in the car.

EXT. PIER – CONTINUOUS

At the end of a pier, in sight of the car park, are Kathy, Ruth and Tommy.

RUTH

It wasn't her. (*Beat.*) Or – I'm not her.

KATHY

. . . No. You aren't.

TOMMY

But it was close, wasn't it? I mean, you could see why Rod and Chrissie thought she might have been a possible.

RUTH

Oh shut up, Tommy. It wasn't close. It wasn't close at all.

An awkward beat.

Then Ruth continues – cold anger growing in her voice.

RUTH

And I knew it wouldn't be her before we even got there. It was never going to be her. They never, ever model us from people like that woman.

KATHY

Ruth – don't –

But Ruth isn't going to stop now.

RUTH

We all know it. We just never say it. We're modelled from trash. Junkies, prostitutes, winos, tramps. Convicts, maybe, so long as they aren't psychos.

Ruth starts to walk back down the pier to the car.

Then stops.

RUTH

If you want to look for possibles, if you want to do it properly, then look in the gutter. That's where we come from.

Ruth leaves Tommy and Kathy alone.

EXT. PIER – SUNSET

At the end of the pier, Kathy is gazing out to sea.

KATHY

We should go back.

Tommy doesn't reply.

He is watching Kathy. The light on her face. The way the wind pulls at her hair.

INT. CAR – EVENING

The sun is going down as they drive through Norfolk, back towards the Cottages.

EXT. COTTAGES – NIGHT

The car pulls up at the Cottages.

INT. COTTAGES – NIGHT

In the hallway of the main house, just past the coat rack, is a featureless metal box, attached to the wall, just like the one in Hailsham.

The front door opens, and Ruth walks straight in.

As she passes the metal box, she swipes it with her bracelet.

Tommy and Kathy follow behind.

INT. KITCHEN – NIGHT

Kathy is cooking over the stove.

A couple of other faces from the Cottages are sitting at the kitchen table, eating their dinner.

Coming from the bedroom, we hear the sound of raised voices.

An argument. Say:

RUTH
(*out of shot*)
I don't know why you'd say something like that. Do you actually want me to get angry?

TOMMY
(*out of shot*)
Of course I don't.

RUTH
(*out of shot*)
Then what do you want? If you don't want to make me angry, if you don't want me to be upset, why would you say something so completely stupid?

We can't fully make out the words, but we can recognise the voices as Ruth and Tommy. It sounds as if Ruth is doing most of the shouting.

People at the dining table look round at the noise, then exchange glances, then go back to whatever they were doing.

INT. FRONT HALL – EARLY MORNING

Kathy sits in the front hall of the Cottages, pulling on a pair of wellington boots.

She then stands, and opens the front door.

It's a beautiful morning outside. The sun is just coming up.

TOMMY

Where are you going?

Kathy turns and sees Tommy, through the open kitchen doorway.

He's at the dining table, on which is spread out a sheet of paper. He is at the early stages of a large drawing.

KATHY

I thought I'd go for a walk.

TOMMY

. . . Does that mean you want to be alone? Or can I come too?

INT. TOMMY'S ROOM – CONTINUOUS

Ruth stands at the window of Tommy's room, peering out of a gap in the curtains . . .

. . . watching Tommy and Kathy walking away from the Cottages.

EXT. COTTAGES/GREENHOUSE – CONTINUOUS

Kathy and Tommy walk through a large greenhouse attached to the cottage complex.

When Tommy speaks, his words are deliberate. Pre-prepared. This is a conversation he has internally rehearsed before now.

TOMMY

Chrissie and Rod are pretty obsessed with this rumour, aren't they?

KATHY

About the deferrals.

Tommy nods.

TOMMY

I was thinking that if this rumour was true, it might explain quite a lot.

KATHY

Such as?

TOMMY

Well – the Gallery for instance. We never got to the bottom of it, what the Gallery was for.

Beat.

TOMMY

Pictures, poetry, sculptures. It tells you something about yourself. That's the point about art, isn't it? It says what's inside you. It reveals your soul.

KATHY

That's what they used to tell us.

TOMMY

Right. (*Beat.*) So – suppose that the rumour is true. A special arrangement has been made for Hailsham students. If they're in love. There would have to be a way to tell if couples are telling the truth, and not just lying to put off their donations.

Beat.

TOMMY

Well, that's what the Gallery would be for. In the Gallery, they can find out everything about us that they need to know. So if we say we're in love, they can look into our souls, and they'll know if it's real love, or just a lie.

Beat.

KATHY

That's a strange idea, Tommy . . .

TOMMY

Is it? I don't see why it's stranger than any other idea.

KATHY

. . . and didn't Miss Lucy tell you that making art for the Gallery wasn't important?

TOMMY

Yes. She did. But look what happened to her.

A moment between Tommy and Kathy.

Looking at each other.

Then:

KATHY

Are you thinking of applying? You and Ruth.

TOMMY

It wouldn't work.

Beat.

KATHY

Why?

On Tommy. Weighing up two possible answers.

Then:

TOMMY

You forget. You had a lot accepted into the Gallery. If I applied, they wouldn't have anything to go on.

Beat.

KATHY

It's all just rumours and theories.

TOMMY

I know. But why else would the guardians have wanted us to work so hard on our art and poetry?

KATHY

I don't know, Tommy. I really don't.

EXT. COTTAGES – NIGHT

The Cottages, under a clear starry sky.

INT. TOMMY'S ROOM – NIGHT

Ruth and Tommy are having sex.

INT. KATHY'S ROOM – CONTINUOUS

Kathy can hear Ruth and Tommy.

She reaches for her Walkman, and puts it on.

For a few moments she is transported.

INT. KATHY'S ROOM – CONTINUOUS

The song ends.

Kathy pulls off the headphones.

Opens her eyes.

Then jolts –

– at the sight of a figure, standing in her doorway.

It's Ruth.

She enters Kathy's bedroom, and quietly closes the door behind her.

Then she pads over to Kathy's bed, and kneels down.

The room is only lit by moonlight, filtering through the window.

Ruth's face, though close to Kathy's, is in shadow.

A strange beat.

Then Ruth speaks.

RUTH

(*quietly*)

I know what you think, Kathy. (*Beat.*) I know you think that you and Tommy would have made a natural couple. And you believe there's a chance that Tommy and I will split up some day. And when we do, perhaps that will be your chance with Tommy. A chance to do it right this time.

Ruth's hand reaches out, and gently brushes against Kathy's hair.

RUTH

(*quietly*)

But the thing is, Kathy, although Tommy really likes you as a friend, he just doesn't see you that way. (*She laughs softly.*) Tommy told me all about the porno magazines. We had quite a laugh about it.

Ruth's voice lowers to a bare whisper . . .

. . . and she puts her mouth so close to Kathy that she is almost kissing Kathy's ear.

RUTH

(*quiet*)

He didn't understand what you were doing. But I did.

A moment later, Ruth stands . . .

. . . then leaves, closing the door softly behind her.

A beat, on Kathy's moonlit face.

Her open eyes.

EXT. COTTAGES – DAY

Keffers carries a box of groceries to the main house, where Kathy is waiting at the front door.

When Keffers hands her the box, Kathy doesn't take it.

KATHY

I want to be a carer.

Keffers looks back at her blankly.

KATHY

It's you I apply to, isn't it?

KEFFERS

Yes.

KATHY

So. I'm applying.

Keffers nods.

KEFFERS

I'll bring you the forms tomorrow, and we can start to process.

Kathy takes the box off Keffers.

EXT. FIELD – EARLY EVENING

Plastic bags. Litter in barbed wire.

KATHY
(*voice-over*)

By the time Ruth and Tommy finally separated, my carer training had already begun, so I was hardly ever at the Cottages.

In the field by the cottages, we can see a figure standing.

Tommy.

He is looking away from the cottages – where we can see Keffers' minibus is parked.

KATHY
(*voice-over*)

It had never occurred to me that our lives, until then so closely interwoven, could unravel and separate with such speed.

EXT. COTTAGES – DAY

Kathy is carrying a suitcase out of the front door to the Cottages –

– towards the open boot of the minibus.

Standing beside the minibus is Keffers.

KATHY
(*voice-over*)
If I had known, maybe I'd have kept tighter hold of them, and not let unseen tides pull us apart.

A Young Man helps her with a second suitcase.

From the doorway of the Cottage, two other young people, a Boy and a Girl, watch them.

Kathy turns back and waves to the two standing in the doorway –

– who wave back, smiling.

Kathy's gaze flicks up to Ruth's window –

– but no one is there. Kathy gets into the minibus.

And Keffers drives her away.

Fade to black.

PART 3: COMPLETION

Fade up to –

EXT. BLOCK OF FLATS – EARLY MORNING

A block of flats in early morning.

INT. KATHY'S FLAT – CONTINUOUS

Kathy, aged twenty-six, is lying on a single bed.

Beside the bed, her alarm is sounding.

Kathy switches it off.

Swings her legs out the side of the bed. Rises to a sitting position. And rubs the sleep out of her eyes.

KATHY
(*voice-over*)
For the most part, being a carer has suited me fine. I can

handle the solitude, the broken sleep, and the constant shuttle from clinic to clinic.

We see around Kathy's flat.

It is spartan, tidy, functional, and gives no indication of a life shared with anyone else.

There is a sense that Kathy only uses her flat for eating an early breakfast, or a late dinner, and sleeping.

The one suggestion of a life outside work and sleep is, lined on a shelf, four desk lamps. Each a different colour.

INT. KATHY'S FLAT – EARLY MORNING

Kathy leans against the counter of her kitchenette, eating cereal, gazing absently out of the window.

KATHY
(*voice-over*)

The true test of a carer is when a donor completes earlier than expected, on the second or even first donation. Many go through the carer training, only to find they aren't cut out for it.

INT. CORRIDOR OUTSIDE KATHY'S FLAT – DAY

Kathy exits her flat, swipes her bracelet on the tracking-system box, and locks the door behind her.

INT. CAR – DAY

Kathy drives along an A-road.

INT. WARD ROOM – DAY

Seen through the doorway, Kathy sits beside a hospital bed.

In the bed is a woman about Kathy's age. Hannah.

Hannah has one eye missing, and has bandages around her abdomen.

Kathy pulls a packet of dark chocolate digestives from a plastic carrier bag.

KATHY

Here you are. Dark chocolate. If you knew how many shops I had to try before I found them . . .

HANNAH

I thought I wasn't allowed to eat so soon before the operation.

Kathy breaks the seal on the packet, and takes one biscuit.

KATHY

You aren't, but I am. And after the operation, you can wolf down the rest of the packet in one go.

INT. DOVER RECOVERY CENTRE/CORRIDOR – CONTINUOUS

Through glass, we see a Male Nurse enter Hannah's ward room.

KATHY

(*voice-over*)

I'd never say I've become immune to the completions. But they are something I am able to live with.

Out of our earshot, Kathy and the Nurse talk for a few moments.

Then Kathy stands, and kisses Hannah on each cheek.

EXT. DOVER RECOVERY CENTRE – DAY

The Dover Recovery Centre is in its own grounds.

It is in countryside, but near enough to a motorway to hear the soft rush of traffic, like wind.

INT. LOUNGE AREA – DAY

Kathy sits on a chair in a lounge area.

A few donor patients sit around watching TV, or playing ping-pong. All are damaged – with eyes, teeth, or limbs missing.

Kathy is dozing, with her head resting to the side.

Observed by one of the patients, a young Female Nurse approaches Kathy.

NURSE

You're Hannah's carer, aren't you?

Kathy stirs, and opens her eyes.

NURSE

Hannah's carer.

KATHY

Yes.

Beat.

Kathy scans the Nurse's face, and understands immediately what she sees.

NURSE

I'm sorry. It's always hard. But there were complications.

KATHY

What kind of complications?

The Nurse's expression remains neutral.

NURSE

Unexpected complications.

Beat.

KATHY

Right.

Kathy stands.

She looks very tired.

KATHY

You need me to sign the release.

NURSE

Please.

Kathy follows the Nurse to the ward desk.

INT. WARD DESK – CONTINUOUS

Kathy stands at the ward desk, filling out the forms that the Nurse puts in front of her.

As Kathy writes:

NURSE

Are you going to leave now? We can quite easily provide you with a bed tonight if you've got a long drive.

This is not a real offer.

KATHY

I can be back home in under two hours.

NURSE

Always better to wake at home, isn't it?

Kathy smiles perfunctorily at the Nurse's polite small talk, and starts on the next form –

– then seems to notice something.

It's on the computer screen just behind the desk.

Kathy swivels the screen in order to read it.

On the screen is a medical information readout, and a small passport-sized photo of Ruth.

NURSE

Is it someone you know?

KATHY

. . . Yes. Actually, we grew up together.

NURSE

Oh.

Beat.

KATHY

How is she?

NURSE

. . . Were you close?

KATHY

Very close as children. Though we haven't seen each other now for nearly a decade.

NURSE

Well, Ruth isn't as strong as we would hope at this stage.

KATHY

(*checking the patient form*)

She's done two donations. (*Looks up.*) You think she'll complete on the third?

Beat.

NURSE

I think she wants to complete. And as you know, when they want to complete, they usually do.

INT. WARD CORRIDOR – CONTINUOUS – DAY

Kathy stands outside a ward room.

She hesitates for a couple of moments.

Then goes in.

INT. RUTH'S WARD ROOM – CONTINUOUS

Kathy enters Ruth's ward room.

The bed is empty.

The room feels very still.

Kathy walks up to the bed. On the bedside table is a glass of water, half full, and an open copy of a novel, the spine bent back to keep its place.

Kathy checks over her shoulder, then opens the bedside-table drawer.

She sees a wristwatch, and some hair-clips . . .

. . . and a single Hailsham token. Kept like a lucky casino chip.

Kathy reacts.

Then shuts the drawer.

Almost as soon as she has done so, Kathy hears a noise.

The toilet in the bathroom flushes.

Kathy turns, and, a moment later, the door to the toilet opens.

Revealing Ruth.

She is struggling slightly to exit the bathroom, because she is having to use a walker in order to stay upright, and it's awkward manoeuvring it past the self-closing door.

So for a moment or two, she doesn't notice Kathy.

Then she has the walker past the door frame.

And looks up.

Then freezes at the sight of Kathy. Momentarily stunned, dislocated.

For a moment, the two women gaze at each other.

Then the moment is broken –

– as a smile breaks over Ruth's face.

RUTH

Kathy.

INT. DOVER RECOVERY CENTRE – SUNSET

Kathy and Ruth walk down a corridor in the Dover Recovery Centre.

Ruth's progress, using her walker, is slow.

RUTH

I've kept tabs on you over the years. (*Beat.*) And Tommy too.

KATHY

What do you hear about Tommy?

RUTH

That he's done his second donation too. And apparently, he's doing very well on it. Apparently, he's in better shape than some after their first donation.

KATHY

Good old Tommy. I'm not surprised.

RUTH

. . . Are you surprised at me? (*Beat.*) I expect I look a bit broken, Kath.

Kathy makes no response.

RUTH

But that's okay. I'm not sure I'd want to survive the third donation anyway. You hear things, don't you?

KATHY

. . . What kind of things?

RUTH

Oh, you know. How maybe, after the fourth donation, even if you've technically completed, you're still conscious in some sort of way. And then you find out there are more donations. Plenty of them. Except there are no more recovery centres, and no more carers. There's just watching, and waiting. Until they switch you off. (*Beat.*) I don't think I fancy that.

Silence.

RUTH

Is it the end of the day already?

Kathy looks up to the sky. The sun is low.

RUTH

It's funny. Over the last few months I've probably thought about you every day. Hoping I'd see you. And actually I felt sure I would. It seemed impossible that I'd complete without seeing you one last time.

Beat.

KATHY

It's not the last time, yet, Ruth. They offered me a bed here. I was planning to stay the night anyway.

EXT. DOVER RECOVERY CENTRE – NIGHT

Half the windows in the Recovery Centre remain lit through the night.

INT. RUTH'S WARD ROOM – DAY

The following morning.

Kathy is peeling an orange, watched by Ruth – who is lying in her bed, propped up on pillows.

Kathy pulls the segments neatly apart, then hands them to Ruth.

Ruth smiles.

RUTH

I knew you'd be a good carer. Your donors are very lucky.

Kathy smiles back.

RUTH

Look – I was lying awake last night, and I suddenly had an idea that we'd take a trip together.

KATHY

Where to?

RUTH

(*casually*)

I didn't much think of where. Just a trip. (*A moment.*) Though a place did occur to me. One of the boys on the next floor was telling me about it. It's near the Kingsfield Recovery Centre.

Kathy reacts slightly to the name Kingsfield.

KATHY

Is it the boat? The one stranded on the beach?

RUTH

You're heard about it too?

KATHY

From a carer who had worked there. (*Beat.*) It's quite a drive from here. Are you sure you're up to it?

RUTH

Quite sure.

Beat.

RUTH
(*gently*)

And do you suppose, if we're driving all that way, we could think about calling in on Tommy? Seeing as he's staying at Kingsfield.

Another beat – then Ruth smiles.

RUTH

I told you I'd been keeping tabs on both of you.

KATHY

Have you seen him?

RUTH

Not since the Cottages.

KATHY

No. Neither have I.

Fade to:

EXT. GATES – DAY

Large, automated cast-iron gates.

A sign reads: 'Kingsfield Recovery Centre'.

The gates start to swing open, and Kathy's car drives through.

INT. CAR – DAY

Kathy drives up towards the main building.

Outside the front doors a group of four people, patients, stand chatting.

Ruth makes a sudden sharp intake of breath.

RUTH

Look. There he is.

One of the figures is Tommy. Older, hair cut short, thinner. But entirely recognisable.

He turns to watch the approaching car.

RUTH

Do you think he's recognised us through the glass?

As if in answer, Tommy lifts his hand, as if shielding his eyes from overhead light, and squints at them.

This sends Ruth into a slight panic.

RUTH

What do we do? Do we get out? No, no, let's not get out.

But Kathy has already opened the door.

We stay in the car with Ruth –

– who watches, like a silent film, as Tommy walks towards Kathy.

Then hugs her.

EXT. KINGSFIELD RECOVERY CENTRE – DAY

Now we are with Tommy and Kathy –

– as Kathy is spun round by Tommy's embrace, so that she now faces Ruth, watching through the car windscreen.

Ruth face is oddly blank, almost frozen, as if she is watching people in a play.

KATHY

(*pulling back*)

Ruth's in the car.

Tommy pulls back from Kathy, and goes to open the passenger door –

– and now it is Kathy's turns to watch through the windscreen, as Tommy leans in and kisses Ruth on each cheek.

It is a different kind of greeting. More restrained. And Kathy can see that.

EXT. NARROW COUNTRY ROAD – DAY

Kathy's car drives down a narrow, winding country road. Almost a dirt-track.

INT. CAR – CONTINUOUS

Kathy drives, with Ruth still in the passenger seat and Tommy in the back seat.

TOMMY

I can't believe I have the two of you here. Does it feel to you like we're back at Hailsham again? Like no time has passed?

KATHY

No. It doesn't.

Tommy laughs.

TOMMY

No, it doesn't at all, does it! It feels really weird. (*Beat.*) But good weird!

He laughs again.

TOMMY

So I suppose you both heard that Hailsham was closed. From what you hear, the only schools left now are like Morningdale. Like battery farms, they say. (*Beat.*) I'm sure it's an exaggeration.

Ruth is looking out of the passenger window a little anxiously, as the narrow road gets rougher and more overgrown.

RUTH

Are you sure this is the right way?

KATHY

Yes. I'm sure.

EXT. NARROW COUNTRY ROAD – DAY

Kathy stops the car.

The dirt-track has come to an end.

Kathy and Tommy exit the car.

Ruth opens her door and peers out.

Again, we see the same slight panic in Ruth as when they arrived at Kingsfield and saw Tommy. It is as if, over the intervening years, all her power and authority has gone.

RUTH

My walker is going to be useless here.

TOMMY

It's okay. We'll help you.

Ruth sees that the way ahead is blocked by a tangled barbed-wire fence.

RUTH

Oh no. No one said anything about this. No one said anything about barbed wire.

TOMMY

Ruth, just relax.

INT. FOREST – DAY

Kathy and Tommy carry Ruth, with one of her arms around each of their shoulders.

Kathy also holds a map.

Ruth is not paralysed – she just has very little power in her legs. But the effort for Tommy and Kathy is considerable.

RUTH

Kath – really, are you absolutely sure –

Kathy snaps slightly.

KATHY

Oh, do be quiet, Ruth. I've already told you I'm sure.

TOMMY

Yes, Ruth. For God's sake.

Ruth closes her mouth, and sinks a little deeper into herself.

EXT. SAND DUNES – DAY

The three of them exit the forest . . .

. . . into sand dunes.

And there, a little way ahead of them, is a boat.

An old fishing vessel – sitting in the dunes as if in a snapshot. Listing slightly. Paint peeling, rusting and rotting.

TOMMY
(*quiet*)
Wow.

EXT. BOAT – DAY

Tommy has climbed on to the boat. Right up to the cabin.

He laughs.

Looks back at Ruth and Kathy, and waves.

Kathy and Ruth are on the banks of the dune that overlooks the boat.

Kathy is standing. Ruth is seated.

Kathy waves back to Tommy, but Ruth doesn't appear to see. Apparently lost in her own thoughts.

EXT. SAND DUNES – DAY

Tommy and Kathy sit beside Ruth on the dune, facing the boat.

TOMMY
Maybe that's what Hailsham looks like now.

Beat.

TOMMY
Do you ever hear, Kath? About the other students from Hailsham?

KATHY

Sometimes.

TOMMY

I heard that Amanda completed on her first donation.

RUTH

I think that happens more than they ever tell us.

KATHY

There's no conspiracy. It does happen sometimes. But it's not common.

Tommy keeps gazing at the boat.

TOMMY

There was a guy, at my centre. He always worried he wouldn't make it past his first donation. But it all turned out fine. He's come through his third now, and he's completely all right. (*Beat.*) It's funny. I don't think I'd have been a good carer. But in a way I think I'm a pretty good donor.

RUTH

Well, it's what we're supposed to be doing, isn't it?

Silence.

Then:

RUTH

I'd like you both to forgive me. I don't expect you to.

A long silence.

None of them look at each other.

Then:

KATHY

. . . Forgive you for what?

RUTH

Keeping you and Tommy apart.

Silence.

RUTH

It should have been you two together. I always knew it, as far back as I can remember. But I kept you apart. It wasn't just because of the rumours about deferrals. It was because I was jealous. You had real love, and I didn't. And –

Ruth takes a breath. This is the truth, and it's hard.

RUTH

I didn't want to be the one that was left alone.

Silence.

RUTH

It's the worst thing I ever did. (*Beat.*) And now I want to put it right.

TOMMY

(*quiet*)

I don't know how you can do that, Ruth.

RUTH

I can. If the two of you get a deferral.

Tears start running down Kathy's face, and she wipes them away quickly.

KATHY

It's too late for that. Way too late. It's stupid to even think about it.

RUTH

It's not too late. Tommy. You tell her.

Tommy says nothing.

RUTH

You'll see. Both of you. I wanted to do this trip because I had something to give you.

Ruth reaches into her pocket and pulls out a crumpled piece of paper.

She hands it to Tommy.

RUTH

It's Madame's address. That's who you apply to. That's who you have to go and see.

TOMMY

... How did you get this?

RUTH

It wasn't easy. But I've had years to think about what I did, and years to work out how to make it better. (*Beat.*) Now it's up to you two.

EXT. BOAT – DAY

A breeze whips up sand around the fishing boat. The tide is coming in, lapping around the wood. Kathy, Tommy and Ruth have gone.

Fade to:

EXTREME CLOSE UP OF A DRAWING

Many thousands of careful pen strokes build up to depict an elephant standing in tall grass.

It is oddly similar to the clumsy drawing that Tommy did as a child. In fact, compositionally it is the same.

But this drawing shows the opposite of clumsiness. If anything, it shows a meticulous care, bordering on obsessive.

And there is something strange about the surface of the elephant. It is drawn as if it is reflective, or metallic.

TOMMY

(*out of shot*)

What do you think?

INT. KINGSFIELD/TOMMY'S WARD ROOM – NIGHT

Kathy sits on the floor of Tommy's room in Kingsfield.

She is surrounded by more of these intricate black and white pictures, all depicting different animals. But the one she holds is of the elephant.

TOMMY

I started doing them when we were in the Cottages. After that trip to find Ruth's possible. I realised, you see. If I was ever going to apply for a deferral, I'd need something to show them. (*Beat.*) I've done hundreds over the years.

KATHY

They're wonderful.

TOMMY

Really? I never showed anyone until now. They were my secret. (*Beat.*) Like you reading those porno magazines.

Kathy looks up.

KATHY

You remember that?

TOMMY

I remember.

KATHY

. . . Ruth said you didn't understand what I was doing.

TOMMY

No. I think *she* didn't understand what you were doing. She thought you were looking at the dirty pictures in order to find out about sex. To find out what you were missing. (*Beat.*) But I knew you were looking for your original.

Beat.

KATHY

I used to get these huge urges to have sex. Sometimes they were so powerful I thought I'd do it with anyone. (*Beat.*) So I thought that had to tell me something. Something about what kind of person I was modelled from. I guessed the magazines would be the most likely place I'd find her.

TOMMY

You know those urges are natural, don't you? Normal. We all had them. You know that now.

KATHY

Yes. I know that now.

EXT. KINGSFIELD RECOVERY CENTRE – NIGHT

Lights glow in Kingsfield.

Through one of the windows, we can see Tommy lying in his bed, and Kathy in the chair beside him, reading to him from a book.

INT. KINGSFIELD/TOMMY'S WARD ROOM – CONTINUOUS

Kathy is reading from One Thousand and One Nights.

KATHY

'I embarked on a ship to the city of El-Basrah, with a company of merchants, and we traversed the sea for many days and nights. Passing island after island, sea to sea, land to land. In each place, we bought and sold, and exchanged merchandise.'

Kathy glances at Tommy as she reads.

KATHY

'Until we arrived at one island like the gardens of paradise, and the master of the ship cast anchor there.'

Kathy looks round at Tommy's face again.

TOMMY

(*quietly*)

Don't stop.

Kathy watches him for a few moments.

Then she puts the book down.

Stands.

And gets into bed.

With her eyes never leaving his face, her hand slips under the sheets towards Tommy.

Then she leans forwards and starts to kiss him.

EXT. DOVER RECOVERY CENTRE – SUNSET

Sun sinking over the Recovery Centre.

EXT. DOVER RECOVERY CENTRE/RUTH'S WARD ROOM – DAY

Ruth sits by her window.

She looks even weaker, skin even greyer, than the last time we saw her.

Kathy sits by her.

KATHY

We're going to do it. (*Beat.*) I thought you should know.

RUTH

You're going to apply.

KATHY

Yes.

Ruth closes her eyes.

RUTH

Good.

EXT. SEAFRONT ROAD – DAY

Kathy is seated on a seafront bench.

She watches elderly people making their way down the promenade.

She holds the address Ruth gave her.

Her gaze is directed at one house in particular.

As she watches, in the background, a tall Nigerian man – George – pushes an old woman on a wheelchair.

The old woman is wrapped and sunk into a blanket, and though we do not see her face, it is in fact Miss Emily.

EXT. KINGSFIELD RECOVERY CENTRE – DAY

Kathy and Tommy walk around the Kingsfield grounds, by a swimming pool which has been filled in with concrete.

KATHY

I checked the address. (*Beat.*) We just go there. Next week, I'll take you for lab tests. I'll sign you out for the whole day. And we'll visit Madame on the way back.

Tommy nods.

TOMMY

If we get this – she gives us the deferral – and she gives us, say, three years, just to ourselves . . . what do we do? Where will we go?

KATHY

I don't know. Maybe they'll send us back to the Cottages. Or maybe they have a separate place for people like us. We'll have to wait and see.

TOMMY

We'll have to decide which of my pictures to take. We'll only take the best. Maybe six or seven or them.

KATHY

Yes.

As they walk, Kathy takes Tommy's hand.

KATHY
(*repeats*)

Yes.

INT. OPERATING CHAMBER

Ruth is strapped to an operating table.

She is surrounded by Surgeons and Nurses, who are operating on her opened torso.

Her eyes are open, but glazed.

Ruth blinks once.

The alarm on the heart-rate monitor starts to sound.

No one takes any notice.

Ruth flatlines.

The operation continues, unaffected.

Concludes.

And the various operating staff finish up. Scrub down. Exit.

Leaving Ruth, her cadaver, on the operating table. Alone.

INT. CAR – DAY

Kathy and Tommy sit in the car –

– looking at a red-brick terraced house.

A woman is outside the house, weeding large terracotta planters in the front garden.

The woman is Madame.

EXT. MADAME'S HOUSE – DAY

Kathy and Tommy approach the front gate.

Madame doesn't appear to notice them.

KATHY

Madame.

Madame starts – and looks up. Confused.

KATHY

Sorry. I didn't mean to startle you. But we were at Hailsham. I'm Kathy. This is Tommy. (*Beat.*) We haven't come to give you any trouble.

MADAME

From Hailsham . . . (*Beat.*) If you haven't come to give me trouble, then why are you here?

TOMMY

We came to talk to you. I've brought you some things. (*He lifts his bag.*) Some things you might want for your Gallery.

A long beat, as Madame gazes at them, head tilted slightly.

Then she nods.

MADAME

Very well, then. Come inside.

INT. MADAME'S HOUSE/LIVING ROOM – DAY

The inside of the house is dark, and Madame doesn't switch on the lights.

Madame ushers Tommy and Kathy into the living room, then disappears.

The living room was once two rooms, with the partition wall removed, now replaced by a sliding screen.

The interior is lit by what light filters through the net curtains.

It reveals a Victorian living room, with period furniture, and a feeling of dust and age.

On one wall are two agit-prop posters, in support of the Hailsham Movement.

Opposite, a large watercolour of Hailsham hangs above the fireplace.

TOMMY

Look.

He indicates the watercolour to Kathy.

They talk quietly.

TOMMY

It's Hailsham. It's the bit around the back of the pond.

KATHY

What do you mean? There's no pond here.

TOMMY

No, the pond's behind you.

Kathy seems slightly taken aback by the irritation in Tommy's voice.

TOMMY

You must be able to remember. If you're round the back, with the pond behind you . . .

KATHY

Yes.

Their quiet exchange is silenced by noise on the far side of the sliding screen: Madame moving about. Then the sliding screen is pulled back –

– but apparently for no purpose. The rear half of the living room, beyond what was once the partition wall, is almost completely in shadow.

With the screen fully pulled back, Madame enters the lit area of the room, and indicates that they should sit.

Madame takes a seat in an armchair beside the fireplace, and Kathy and Tommy sit on the sofa opposite.

As they get comfortable, there is a soft mechanical whirring sound from the dark half of the living room, which Kathy is distracted by.

Then brought back to focus by Madame.

MADAME

So.

Long beat.

Then:

TOMMY

We're in love.

Tommy turns to Kathy. then back to Madame.

TOMMY

We're in love. True love. Verifiable.

KATHY

We would never have bothered you if we weren't really sure.

MADAME

Verifiable. I see. (*Beat.*) Go on.

TOMMY

Well, we'd heard about the deferrals. And we'd worked out the purpose of the Gallery.

MADAME

Tell me the purpose.

TOMMY

To use our art from Hailsham to look into our souls, which would verify that we deserved a deferral.

Madame does not react.

TOMMY

The trouble is, I was a bit mixed up in those days. I didn't really do any art, so you never took anything. I know that's my fault, and it's probably much too late . . .

He reaches down and opens his bag.

TOMMY

. . . but I brought some things with me now.

He starts to lay the drawings out on the floor for Madame to see.

TOMMY

Some were done quite recently, but a lot of them are several years old, so there's a spread. And you should have Kath's stuff already. She got plenty into the Gallery, didn't you, Kath?

On Kathy –

– looking at Madame.

She's a step ahead of Tommy. Realising the mistake that she and Tommy have made. Perhaps because, deep down, she already knew.

MADAME

I'm sorry. (*Beat.*) *Je ne saix pas quoi faire.* I never know what to do at this point. Should I let them continue, or should I stop them now?

Silence.

It takes a moment to realise that this question was not asked to the ether, but was directed at someone in particular.

Someone actually in the room, who has not yet been revealed.

MADAME

Well?

Beat.

MADAME

It's you they've really come to see.

VOICE

I suppose it is.

The voice has come from the darkness at the rear of the living room.

And from that darkness now comes the metallic whirring again. A wheel turning.

VOICE

I'll take it from here.

A moment later, out of the darkness, Miss Emily appears.

A shrunken figure, pushed forwards on a wheelchair by her nurse, George.

MISS EMILY

Leave us, George. I'll call when I'm done.

George turns and goes.

A moment between Miss Emily, Kathy and Tommy.

Kathy and Tommy are frozen with surprise.

MISS EMILY

Kathy H and Tommy D. I remember you both. Kathy, a bright girl, and so creative. Tommy, a big heart. And terrible rages.

Tommy remains motionless, holding one his drawings in his hand.

MISS EMILY

We used to get two or three couples like you a year. But not so much these days. (*Beat.*) You're the first for quite a while.

Tommy still doesn't quite understand.

TOMMY

To apply for a deferral.

KATHY

(*quiet*)

There are no deferrals, Tommy.

Tommy looks at Kathy, uncomprehending.

Then back at Madame. Who gently confirms.

MADAME

There are no deferrals. And there never have been.

Beat.

MISS EMILY

We didn't have the Gallery in order to look into your souls. We had the Gallery in order to see if you had souls at all.

In the silence, Madame stands.

She goes to the Hailsham watercolour above the fireplace, and gazes at it a moment.

MISS EMILY

Hailsham was the last place to consider the ethics of donation. We used your art to show what you were capable of. To show that donor children were all but human. But it was all a mistake. We were providing an answer to a question that no one was asking.

Miss Emily glances at Madame.

Then back to Tommy and Kathy.

MISS EMILY

You have to understand. Cancer used to kill almost everyone. Now it kills no one at all. (*Beat.*) You see, it's not an ethical issue. It's just about the way we are. If you ask people to return to darkness, the days of lung cancer, and breast cancer, and motor neurone disease . . . (*She shrugs.*) They simply say no.

Beat.

MISS EMILY

Do you understand?

KATHY

Yes.

Madame turns to Tommy.

MADAME

Your drawings are very good. If you want, I'll keep them.

Tommy doesn't answer.

He just stares blankly into space.

EXT. MADAME'S HOUSE – DAY

Tommy and Kathy leave Madame's house.

Tommy walks ahead of Kathy, straight to the car parked outside, and gets inside.

Kathy pauses at the doorway, where Madame stands.

KATHY

Thank you for talking to us.

Madame says nothing.

Beat.

KATHY

I know what you're thinking.

Madame reacts, slightly dreamily, as if she has momentarily lost focus.

MADAME

Tell me.

KATHY

There was a time you saw me. It was one afternoon, in the dormitories. There was no one else around, and I was playing this tape. This music.

Madame smiles distantly.

MADAME

Yes. (*Beat.*) I still think about that occasion from time to time.

KATHY

. . . So do I.

A beat.

Then Madame reaches out, and touches Kathy's cheek.

MADAME

You poor creatures. I wish I could help you. But you're by yourselves now.

INT. CAR – EARLY EVENING

Kathy and Tommy drive in silence through countryside, back towards Kingsfield.

Shadows are long. The countryside is bathed in the last of the day's sunlight.

Fields line the road on either side.

TOMMY

Could you stop the car? I'm sorry. I need to get out a minute.

Kathy turns to Tommy, but Tommy is looking directly ahead, his gaze fixed on an indeterminate point.

Kathy slows the car, pulls over to the side of the road.

They stop on a small grass verge.

Without saying another word, Tommy gets out of the car, and shuts the door behind him.

Leaving Kathy in a little bubble of silence.

She watches as Tommy walks a short way down the road.

Then stops, caught in the glare of the headlights.

Then, just as he did as young boy, on the playing field –

– he throws his head back and starts to scream at the sky.

Insulated from the sound, Kathy watches.

Then she opens the door.

EXT. CAR – CONTINUOUS

Kathy walks to Tommy.

Kathy and Tommy stand by Kathy's car.

They embrace, holding each other tightly for several moments.

Eventually, fade to:

INT. HAILSHAM – DAY

Kathy, twelve, sits in the art room.

She sees Tommy, studiously working on his drawing.

Sees Ruth, working on her own drawing.

She watches them for several moments. In the afternoon sunshine. The tree-tops moving in the wind outside the art-room windows.

Then Tommy looks up at Kathy and smiles.

KATHY
(*voice-over*)
Tommy completed on his fourth donation.

Cut to:

EXT. ROAD – DAY

Kathy's car is driving along an empty road.

KATHY
(*voice-over*)
I've been given my notice now. My first donation is in six weeks.

INT. CAR – DAY

Kathy isn't sobbing, but her eyes are filling with tears.

KATHY
(*voice-over*)
What I'm not sure about is whether our lives have been so different from the lives of the people we save. We all complete.

She pulls over to the side of the road, and gets out of the car.

EXT. ROAD – DAY

Kathy stands by the roadside, collecting herself.

By the road are fences, lining the fields.

And caught in the barbed wire . . .

. . . are hundreds of abandoned plastic bags.

KATHY
(*voice-over*)
And none of us really understand what we've lived through. Or feel we've had enough time.

End.